The
People Mover

The Secret to Effortless Faith

KELLY DYKSTRA

Thrill & Move
worldwide

Thrill & Move Worldwide
Otsego, Minnesota 55330

The People Mover: The Secret to Effortless Faith
Copyright © 2015 by Kelly Dykstra

www.kellydykstra.com

Cover design by Angie Carlson
Author photo by Holland Dykstra

ISBN: 0996022325
ISBN-13: 978-0996022323

DEDICATION

The People Mover is dedicated to the
staff of The Crossing Church.

That you would choose to do this life with us means
you're either unbelievably special or profoundly crazy.

I love how each of you are so uniquely wired by God to
play your part. It's incredible getting to be a part of your
faith journey and watching you thrive.

Thank you for growing along with us,
for your grace along the way,
and for being so much fun.

KELLY DYKSTRA

WHAT'S IN THIS BOOK

FOREWORD

I grew up in Mississippi where "off-roading" was a normal weekend activity. In fact, this sport took on club status and often became the domain of a select group of guys. Basically, this sport was not a sport at all. It was simply taking your pick-up truck off the road and blazing your own trail through the underbrush, over hills and around ravines.

Off-roading was even better after a rain, because there was the skid factor and the mud to add to the challenge. I kid you not, many guys I knew rated their girlfriends on how much they enjoyed hanging on for dear life in a pick-up truck in a race to beat Bobby Joe to the water tank, without the benefit of a road!

And, before you ask, yes, I participated. You may question the thrill of the bone-jarring bouncing over field terraces and the bruising landings after crashing into unseen ditches, but remember, this was before video games. We lived outside, and we lived out loud! But, I will say, there was always a tiny sigh of relief when I drove back onto Highway 57 with no major injuries to my vehicle or myself.

What I remember most vividly was the marked difference between forging my own path "cross country" and driving down the road that someone before me had blazed, cut and paved. Once on the road, my ride became smooth. I could actually move forward without wondering if I would break my truck or myself. And I could pick up speed, which was virtually impossible off-road. Driving became easy. Years before, the county engineers and contractors had done the work, and I now had a clear and open road.

Often it seems our faith parallels that struggle. We think the more we do on our own, the better we must be. We push and we grab. We climb and we fight. We have bone jarring bounces and bruising landings, and still we stay "off road".

In her inspiring and captivating book, *The People Mover*, Kelly Dykstra shares the clear and open way to get on the smooth road. Her years of ministry and of participating fully in life have given her great insight into how to stop trying and start trusting. This book will bless you with a fresh look at scripture, and you will see, woven throughout the Bible, God's desire and preparation for your road of faith.

When I first met Kelly, I was impressed with her zest for life and her devotion to her family and church. These traits are readily seen throughout *The People Mover* as Kelly draws from her personal experiences to express the beautiful confidence and the incredible benefits of a life of faith.

This book will make you feel as if you and Kelly are in a conversation. So, find a comfortable chair, grab a cup of coffee and enjoy this chat with a new friend who so clearly shares the heart of God.

And if you are ever in south Mississippi, try off-roading. You just might be thrilled!

-- Dr. Dave Martin, America's #1 Christian Success Coach and author of *The 12 Traits of the Greats*

1

THE AIRPORT ADVENTURE

So here's what happened

A while back, Eric and I were traveling from Minneapolis to Houston on a Sunday night. We had a brief layover scheduled in Chicago, and as we were packing and preparing to leave during one of the most exhausted times of our week (Sundays are so draining in our line of work), I was looking forward to a nice airport "dinner date" with my favorite guy during that stop. I was thinking, *I'll get packed, get the kiddos squared away, we'll get to the airport, and when we hit Chicago, we'll sit and look at each other and have a lovely meal.*

Well, that didn't happen. Our plane showed up about an hour late to Minneapolis, landing us in Chicago about 10 minutes before our next flight was to depart. There wouldn't be another flight that would get us to Houston that night, and we had an 8:30 appointment the next morning. So we exploded out of the jet way and started running.

Our next gate was in a different concourse.

Naturally, the airport was packed.

And I was wearing heels.

Don't judge me.

Running side-by-side in a crowded airport is challenging, so I told Eric, "I'll follow you," thinking he would clear the way for me. Not so. He was weaving in and out of traffic like a running back with the ball. Spin this way, jump that way, elbow some dude in the gut—just kidding. He wasn't quite that bad, but close. And every 30 seconds or so, he'd turn around and look for me like, "Why can't you keep up?"

Really.

Now, I wear heels a lot. I can run in them just fine. But I was wearing a pair that you have to grip with your toes when you run. It was getting painful.

So I did the unthinkable.

I took my shoes off and ran *barefoot* through the airport.

I'm the girl who brings a pair of socks to put on to go through security, and then turns them inside out when I return them to my bag, so the germs don't touch anything.

There I was, sprinting through the crowd, trying not to run over anyone, dragging my red roller bag, my poor feet picking up bacteria from countless countries. I was sweating, my hair was flying everywhere, and I was feeling a little desperate.

God, help me.

And then I saw it.

Rose-colored light shone from heaven, sprinkling flecks of pure gold to guide the way to the answer to my pathetic plea for relief.

The People Mover.

In that moment, I had a choice.

I could continue how I was. I could run on, trusting my own short legs, out-of-shape heart and sweaty effort to get me to my gate and on my way to my destination.

Or I could shift directions for a second and jump on to something that *just might* make my life easier and propel me to where I needed to go.

My mama didn't raise no dummy.

I fought my way diagonally to my right and hopped on. Now, I wasn't able to just stand—I had no time for that in my particular situation—but I jogged along and let the Mover take me where I needed to go, faster than I could have gone alone.

I didn't have to worry about running into people because they were all going the same direction as me, and they followed the guide on the belt that said "STAND" on the right side, and "WALK" on the left.

I cruised through the concourse on the People Mover, shooting out the other end and miraculously making it to my flight and my ultimate destiny—I mean, *destination*.

That's life

Later, when I had time to think, I realized that my airport adventure looked a lot like life.

We think we're on our way, we have plans, hopes, dreams; then we get delayed or diverted, and obstacles crowd our route. Then God shows us there's a better way to live. But the choice is up to us. Keep fighting along or hop on the People Mover.

I'm reminded of that verse where Jesus said, *I am the way, the truth and the life. No one comes to the Father except through Me.* (John 14:6)

I always thought the real point of this verse was the second half. No one can be "saved" except through Jesus' finished work on the cross. He's the one that makes it happen. Nothing added to or subtracted from this plan works. No other religion gets you in. No other method gets you salvation or heaven. No one comes to the Father except through Jesus. It's a good verse. It helps when presenting salvation to someone or arguing that Christianity is the *only way*.

But I spent too many years sliding past the first part of that verse. Holy moly. What if we focused on the first part? "I AM the way," He says.

The great theologian Steven Tyler made famous the words, "Walk this way!" Can't you just hear his scratchy awesome voice? "Walk this way!" Go ahead. Stop for a second and sing it with me, in your best rocker voice: "Walk this way!" [If you're in Starbucks, just smile and nod at all the people who looked at you funny.]

I guess I thought of the first part of that verse like Jesus pointing to the road to Heaven, saying, "Walk this way!" And then my job as a Christian is to follow Him and walk the narrow path without falling off.

But Jesus says I AM the way.

He is ACTUALLY the way.

Jesus is the People Mover.

He doesn't point the way toward the People Mover or stand beside it to throw us on, or hang out at the end to welcome us home. He doesn't say, "Go that way." He IS the WAY. He IS the TRUTH by which we live. He IS the LIFE that holds our very existence.

Jesus IS the People Mover!

What if life in faith isn't about finding the right way or keeping the rules or serving God with the right amount of commitment or giving sacrificially enough or denying yourself all pleasure or praying for a certain number of hours or fasting, or...or...or... all the things we think the Christian life is about?

What if a relationship with God is as simple as stepping onto the People Mover each day and cruising along in His grace, power, wisdom, truth, life?

What if faith is simpler than you think?

What if it was almost...effortless?

Stick around. I'll tell you what I have come to believe. It's what works for me. Hear me out, and then you can decide for yourself.

Prayer

Jesus, You are the way, truth, and life.

Please open my heart and mind to what You want to teach me as I read this book.

Help me discern which parts are for me, and what parts are not.

In Your name, Jesus, I bind enemy spirits/lies that would cause me to miss the change You wish to work in me.

I look forward to new joy as I explore Your grace and truth.

Amen.

2

A CHANGE IN THINKING

It's all in your head

What if faith could feel effortless?

Is it possible?

Well, if you *think* it's hard or complicated or exhausting, the idea of *effortless* might sound implausible. But maybe it could be...really good. How do you get from a complicated view of the Christian walk to a refreshingly effortless life of faith?

It would start by changing your thinking.

After all, change starts in the mind.

Romans 12:2 says, *Do not be conformed to the pattern of this world, but be transformed by the renewing of your mind.*

What is the pattern of this world? Well, it's a lot like me (and the rest of the crowd) fighting our way through the concourse in Chicago's Midway airport. We carry baggage and hold tickets –ideas– to where we think we need to go. We look around for directions.

To the screens that say what's up.

What's coming and going, when and where and how soon and how late.

We face delays and bad weather and security (or insecurity) issues.

We find people who are helpful and point out where they think we need to be, and we buy overpriced provisions for the trip and guilty-pleasure gossip mags and we lay toilet paper on the seats and panic when our phones are dying and fight for the coveted spots by the power outlets.

We treat ourselves to Starbucks and then worry that we'll have to use the bathroom on the plane.

There's little rest for the weary.

It's each man for himself. Each woman for herself.

If we are traveling with children, we hope to goodness that they won't cry or pitch a fit or cause problems, or (God forbid) run off.

We hope mean people won't judge us, and we pretend not to notice when someone harasses the gate agent.

We pray for safe travels, and we try not to worry about missing the connections that won't wait for us.

What if...what then...

These questions and worries bump around in the back of our brains as we rush through life hoping we can just get it right.

It is the pattern of the airport.

It is the pattern of *this world.*

Romans 1:21 paints a picture of those living according to the pattern of this world [my notes in brackets].

Yes, they knew God, [that He existed]

but they wouldn't worship him as God [acknowledge that He had power to BE GOD in their lives] or even give Him thanks.

And they began to think up [under the influence of enemy lies]

foolish ideas of what God was like [lies about God's heart for His children].

As a result, their minds became dark and confused.

Would you agree with me that our world is full of people whose minds are dark and confused?

Would you agree that sometimes, it's you?

Sometimes, it is me.

Let's play "have you ever..."

Have you ever found yourself racing through life, trying to get where you need to go, doing everything you know to do, fighting obstacles and people and trying to follow signs and not miss your turns? Maybe your wife, husband, friend, or leader, who always seems to be ahead of you, keeps looking back, saying, "Come on!"

You're trying hard to keep up, but you're dragging baggage and you're wearing the wrong shoes and your hair's in your face and you're starting to sweat.

You've heard that it's a good idea to take care of yourself, so you pause for a moment to regroup, remove your jacket, and free yourself from your painful shoes. But then you take a deep breath and run on.

Your destination—your destiny—your dream—calls to you, but you're not sure if you'll ever get there. And while you're running, you're stressed out, worried that you won't make it, and you'll just get stuck in the place where you are, missing opportunities because you just couldn't keep pace with all the expectations.

God, help me.

You might even look over and see some people on the People Mover. They look pretty happy, and they sure aren't sweating like you. They're just cruising along, some standing, some walking, some even jogging, and you think about how it must feel to have that kind of power under your feet.

But you think, *well, good for them. I'm glad they've found something that works for them.*

That People Mover sure looks like it helps people.

One of the People Mover people might even see you struggling and wave you over, but you just give him the thumbs up, because there's no way you could get where you need to go by just standing there like he is.

Surely there's more to it than that.

It probably costs something to ride that thing, and you might need your cash when you get where you're hoping to go.

So you just keep praying and running on your own. You plot your course. *I'll continue for a few more yards and then go around that newsstand and cut through the college group and past the grandma...then I'll stop and check the screens to be sure my gate hasn't changed.*

The more you think about it, the more you think you'd really like access to a People Mover. It would sure be nice to have access to some kind of power that could help you get where you need to go.

There's an opening just ahead. Something compels you to give it a try. But that would mean a slight shift in direction, and what if it made you look weak or got you rejected? Then you've lost your forward momentum.

So you work up a plan of your own. Maybe if you work hard enough and run fast enough and pray hard enough, a People Mover of your own will suddenly appear under your feet. God will somehow decide that you're doing a good enough job on your own that He'll help you out.

I'm here to pop that bubble for you, and I don't even feel bad about it.

Just like the airport architect didn't suddenly come running and design a People Mover under my feet as I struggled through the concourse, God is not going to suddenly show up where you're trying to make it in your own human effort--and grant you His power.

You have to CHOOSE to get on the People Mover that He already put in place.

Are you talking to ME?

I'm talking to two kinds of people here.

First, you who haven't yet chosen to give your life over to the care and leadership of Jesus. Jesus Christ paid for your ride through life on the People Mover of His grace and power.

His death gives you life.

He struggled so you wouldn't have to.

He took God's wrath so you could receive His pleasure.

Why not step into it?

I've heard many preachers say something like this, "When you choose to follow Jesus, it won't be all rainbows and unicorns. Being a Christian will make people hate you, and you'll walk a hard road. But—true story—you'll get heaven when you die!"

Remarkably, some people choose faith anyway, because, despite the flaws of us Christians and our failure to adequately understand or explain *God*, He still draws people to Himself!

I hope that despite the flaws in this book, God will draw

you to Himself. I hope you see that following God doesn't simply secure you a fire insurance policy (from hell), but a People Mover plan to a custom-made purposeful life.

After all, joining forces with the Designer of your destiny on earth and experiencing the full life He created for you is way more attractive than sitting around waiting to die.

The second group of people I'm talking to is the Christians who miss what the People Mover offers. You truly believe that Jesus paid for your trip to Heaven ("By grace you are saved through faith...it is the gift of God," etc.), but somewhere along the line you began to believe that after your salvation, you were then left to fight your way through a hard life until you (blessedly) get to die and arrive at your destination!

Walk with me here. Soooo...if your line of thinking holds true, the only difference between you as a Christian and the rest of the world is that you believe you know how your story ultimately ends. Until then, your success; your life path; your achievement; it's all up to you.

Human effort.

You think you receive "salvation" and simultaneously get handed a carry-on full of rules and are then sent off to have a "successful" Christian life.

If this is your mindset, at some point you'll find yourself

sweaty and exhausted, trying to follow the right people and get where you think you should go.

Recently, I caught up with an old friend whose teenager is dealing with some typical teen angst. She said she told him, "You know what? Life is hard!"

The warning bells went off in my head.

Why? After all, haven't I said that myself? "Life is hard." Or, on a particularly bad day, "Life is hard, and then you die."

What if that's a lie?

What if life isn't hard?

Or at least, what if you changed your thinking and simply decided your life wasn't going to be hard?

Maybe I'm messing with your brain a little here, but hang with me. What if you could CHANGE YOUR THINKING and make your own life NOT HARD?

What if a life of faith is easier than you think?

Romans 12:2 says, *Do not be conformed to the pattern of this world, but be transformed by the renewing of your mind.*

If you'd like to see positive change in your life, it begins with a change in your thinking. A renewing of the mind. Let's talk about a shift in thinking that could lead you to a life that is elevated above the pattern that so many of our fellow humans fall into—of human effort; the human struggle to get by.

I mean, really, if God TELLS you to not be *conformed* to this world's patterns, but be *transformed* by changing your thinking, couldn't you expect that your life should be somehow different from the average Joe?

In fact, shouldn't it be way, way better than average?

***

What if you saw your life—every single day—as a choice between a) fighting your way down the concourse, and b) riding on the People Mover?

I want to challenge you–Christian or not—to choose to hook up with Jesus, the People Mover. Over the course of this book, I'd like to show you what I've learned about the goodness of God and the benefits of stepping out of the exhausting struggle so many call living, and into this surprisingly effortless journey of faith.

Prayer for a New Believer

Jesus, I have spent my life rejecting You and ignoring the price You paid so that I could live. I believe You are God, that You died to pay for my sins, and that You were raised to life so I might live in victory.

I receive Your forgiveness and ask You to lead my life. I step onto the People Mover today and submit my way to You.

In Your name, Jesus, amen.

Prayer for an Old Believer

Jesus, I've asked You to forgive my sins and lead my life. I trust You for a place in heaven when my earthly life is done.

But somewhere along the line, I believed the lie that I have to work my way through life in order to make God happy with me or to be successful in Your eyes.

I reject that lie, receive Your forgiveness once again for trying to achieve my own success, and step onto You, the People Mover.

Please help me remain IN You. I believe that You will take great care of me and carry me to better places than I ever dreamed.

I pray in Your name Jesus, amen.

KELLY DYKSTRA

3

RETURN TO THE GARDEN

What makes us think we can figure out how to make it in life without God? Surely we know we're human? "What can I say? I'm only human!" is our excuse for any screw-ups. Yet we refuse to give up control to a Higher Power! What's up with that?

Well, it goes back to the original sin. (Don't worry; this chapter has a good ending.)

History lesson

Let's go way back. In Genesis, the Bible tells the story of

Eve, who was tempted to sin. You know the story, but don't skip through this because I think it's good stuff. We enter the story where Satan (the serpent) is dangling the carrot—um—fruit, in front of Eve.

> Genesis 3:4-6, *"You won't die!" the serpent replied to the woman. "God knows that your eyes will be opened as soon as you eat it, and you will be like God, knowing both good and evil." The woman was convinced. She saw that the tree was beautiful and its fruit looked delicious, and she wanted the wisdom it would give her.*

Do you see what motivated her sin? Not just the appealing nature of the fruit. (I don't know about you, but if it was about taste, I think *bacon* would have been more effective a temptation.) It wasn't even that she wanted to rebel against God. It was a desire to get her *own* wisdom apart from God's plan. To achieve her *own* understanding of right and wrong.

See, prior to this choice, Adam and Eve lived in innocent faith in God, His friendship, His provision, and the work He provided for them to do.

Their work occupied them; it didn't provide for them.

It gave them purpose, but not provision.

All their provision came from God. It was a life of faith

and rest. Friendship and productivity. Beauty and innocence.

The only caution that God gave them was, "Do this life My way, and don't try to achieve your own wisdom or accomplishment." He included a little bit of tension in Eden. He could have eliminated all options and forced them to be His friends forever, but He gave them the ability to opt-out of the faith/rest life if they wanted to. Who really values a forced friendship? He left it up to them.

And then. Epic fail.

Here's how it went down, in Genesis 3:7. *At that moment their eyes were opened, and they suddenly felt shame at their nakedness. So they sewed fig leaves together to cover themselves.*

The moment they opted out, their eyes were opened to their own discernment of good and evil. They saw themselves as God saw them: unholy in the eyes of a holy God. Up until this point, their faith in Him caused Him to overlook their humanness. But the second they abandoned their faith and chose to take control, they were on their own.

They were exposed. Innocence was gone. So they attempted to [literally] cover their butts. They started working to protect themselves—making clothes and hiding in the bushes.

God showed up. The blame game began. The curse of conflict, pain and toil settled heavily on the shoulders of humankind. No longer was provision freely offered; it had to be achieved by the sweat of the brow. No longer was simple faith enough; now humans had to use their judgment to get along with each other and survive. The results were disastrous. (Have you read the Old Testament? Ugh.)

Before Adam and Eve were banished, God did a final cool thing. He made them clothing from animal skins. He sacrificed an animal on their behalf, to cover and protect them. It was a picture of Jesus, who would, thousands of years later, be sacrificed to cover the epic fail they made that day, the epic fails we make today, and all the epic fails in between and ever after.

Back to the future

Each day, you have a choice. You wake up with the carrot/fruit dangling in front of your own face. Do you reach for it, take a bite and say, "I've got this," and proceed to get to work, covering your un-holiness, compensating for your humanness, condemning others who don't get it right either, and slaving away for your provision? When you step out of bed, does the curse settle heavily on your shoulders?

Or…do you punch the serpent in the face, push away the temptation of human effort and say, "Thank you, Jesus."

He sacrificed Himself for you. Do you acknowledge that He took your punishment so God would once again overlook your un-holiness? Because of Jesus, you can once again (like in the Garden), live in innocence and complete faith that your Father God walks and talks with you. He provides everything, and your daily work is motivated by a fulfillment of purpose, not a scramble for provision.

It's a re-*new*-ing of the mind. Like, the original mind of humankind.

A return to when the world was new. A return to God's original desire for the God/people dynamic. When people and God walked hand-in-hand because they trusted Him for everything.

You're not forced; you have a choice.

After Adam and Eve's epic fail, the line was clearly drawn, separating them from God. They had to figure it out on their own. But because of Jesus, you have an opt-in to a life of faith and rest. Will you take it? Not just once, but will you opt-in every day for the rest of your life?

Your faith in His work covers your un-holiness and allows you to live in friendship with your Creator and the lover of your soul.

Jesus.

He died to reverse the curse.

He died that the weight would be lifted.

He died that we might be restored to an intimate relationship with God.

That we may re-enter a life of faith and rest .

That in the middle of our crazy world, we have a Garden of Eden sanctuary for our souls.

That we might walk with Him each day without the obstacle of our un-holiness and shame.

There is no need to cover ourselves. We are covered.

There is no need to struggle and work in our own wisdom and effort.

Once again, we can innocently trust Him.

We go to work each day to live out our purpose; not to eke out our provision. He is our supply.

It is a renewing of our minds. A return to the like-new state of the mind of humankind.

Because of Jesus.

Prayer

God, the temptation to wake each day and take control is so strong.

Let me not even open my eyes without gratitude for Jesus' sacrifice that grants me friendship with You. I work in Your power, that I may bring good to the world. I do not struggle or strive. I do not live under a curse. My un-holiness is covered, and I live in rest and faith in You, my Creator.

Because of Jesus, amen.

4

BENEFIT 1:
THE WILL OF GOD AIN'T HARD TO FIND

The next few chapters will focus on some specific benefits that become yours when you choose to let God renew your mind and transform you from a human-effort mentality to complete trust in the People Mover (Jesus). The first benefit is one of my favorites, because it takes the stress out of my perfectionist/must-get-it-right mind.

God's super-secret will

When you get on the People Mover, you line yourself up with God's perfect plan for your life. All my life, I've heard about the elusive (cue important music: *bom bom BOOOOM*) **"WILL OF GOD"**. There are books and sermons and lectures and study groups centered around "finding the **Will Of God** for your life." Like it's some mysterious code you can crack. There's probably going to be a movie about it some day, probably starring Nick Cage or Brendan Fraser. *The Adventures of Finding the **Will of God**.*

The will of God.

Christians fear missing it. And everybody knows if you miss it and take a wrong turn, you're up the proverbial creek without the proverbial paddle. (Have you ever noticed that if you're "up" a creek without a paddle, you can always just float back down? In my opinion, it's far worse to be "down" a creek without a paddle. Because then you have to get out and push your canoe back up. Just sayin'.)

Well, if you get up each day and step onto the People Mover, submitting fresh each morning to whatever Jesus wants to do with you that day, and trusting His power to propel you there, won't you be OK? I mean, the Bible says we as believers have the mind of Christ (1 Corinthians 2:16). If you actually *believe* that, and you keep an ongoing conversation with Him throughout each day, won't the right decisions naturally happen? Won't He help you stay within the plexi-glass walls of His design for you, and carry you forward where He wants you to go?

Call this a Pollyanna (incurable optimist) version of life in faith, but in the end, the Pollyannas are happy, they help people, the people help them back in hard times, and they get movies made about them. I suppose Scrooges get movies made about them too, but only because of the change of heart involved.

Anyway.

The Conveyor Belt

Think about this.

OK, so a People Mover is a giant version of tank treads or a conveyor belt at the grocery store checkout, right? It's cyclical. It goes to the end, circles under, comes back, and goes to the end again, and circles back. I put a jar of olives on the belt; it travels to the end of its little journey, and is delivered to the cashier. Meanwhile, the belt has traveled back underneath, to the beginning to get the rest of my stuff.

It's never *not* at the beginning, middle, and end, all at the same time.

Not to over-simplify deep theology, but I think the conveyor belt concept is kind of like God and His version of time. He is not confined to our ability to only occupy this moment right now. He is not guessing what's coming down the road. He has already been down the road, to the end, circled back, and is where you are.

He *is* the road. He is Alpha and Omega, the beginning and the end. He *was* and *is* and *is to come* (Revelation 4:8). God has planned out the entire scope of your life. He has a vision for your future!

Jeremiah 29:11 says, *"For I know the plans I have for you," says the Lord. "They are plans for good and not for disaster, to give you a future and a hope."*

God has been to your future. He declares that it is GOOD, and He has circled back around to get you and take you there!

This means that God knows every bump in your road. He knows every obstacle, every opportunity, every difficult choice you'll need to make. He knows ahead of time that you'll have (what you perceive as) a delay or a closed door. He also knows when the door will be kicked open and your breakthrough will happen.

He's been there and done that, and He says, "Jump on with me! Let me take you to your destiny!" When you can't see past a problem that has reared its ugly head, God's not biting His nails, wondering how it's going to turn out.

He says, "I've already seen this place. I've got this. Stay with it. Stay with me."

The Right Path

I am notoriously bad at directions. Not just driving. Like, when I am staying at a hotel, I am famous for walking out of my room and instinctively turning the wrong direction. When I step off an elevator, nine times out of ten, I will go the wrong way down the hall. Eric thinks this is hilarious. He will intentionally pause and let me step out ahead of him. Then he'll just stand there to see how long it takes me to realize I've gone wrong, and I turn around and see him smirking back by the elevator.

God will let you take the lead in your life—if you want to—but the second you realize you've gone the wrong way, He'll be right there to get you back on track. You'll never see Him standing way back down the hall smirking at you. You won't feel His condemnation. You might project condemnation on yourself, but He's not giving it. There is NO condemnation for those who belong to Christ Jesus. (Romans 8:1). Nope, He will just graciously say, "Are you ready for me to take the lead now?"

Because of my directional issues, I dislike finding my way around in strange places. I really like letting Eric lead, because his navigating instincts are good. The best-case scenario is when he goes exploring and finds his way around wherever we are visiting, and then he comes back to get me. We were in Florida last year, and he had checked into our resort before I arrived. It was so lovely to be dropped off at the entrance and have my husband confidently guide me through the labyrinth of the resort. I didn't have to read signs or ask for help. I just enjoyed the view of the lovely place, and followed him.

When you're living in the care of the People Mover, you're in the company of Someone who loves you and has already explored where you're going. You can simply follow His lead without fear of your instincts being wrong. His are always good, and He promises that He will infuse you with His wisdom to move forward on a good path.

Proverbs 3:5-6 says, *Trust in the Lord with all your heart; do not depend on your own understanding. Seek His will in all you do, and He will show you which path to take.*

1 Corinthians 2:16 confirms, *Who can know the Lord's thoughts? ...But we understand these things. For we have the mind of Christ.*

When there's a fork in the road of your life, and you must make a choice, if the eyes of your heart are on Him, and you're resting in His ability to take you where you need to go, you can trust that your decisions will be right.

When you get on the People Mover, there's no stress

about missing something God has for you. There's no second-guessing or guilt over choices made while truly seeking to follow Him. I'm not talking about sin issues here. If you make a choice to deliberately defy God by disobeying scripture or behaving in a way that is *not* in line with His character and heart for you, you've left Him back at the elevator, and you need to choose to step back in line with God.

But if you simply do your best each day to align yourself with Him, ask Him to show you His paths for you, you can make the choices as they arise and trust that He will work out His plan in you. He speaks to us in a variety of ways—through scripture, in prayer, circumstances He lines up, and through wise pastors/friends. Ask, listen, and check whether the answer lines up with Bible truth. Then go ahead and move.

No more woulda-shoulda-coulda

Honestly, sometimes I look back at a choice I made and think, "Maybe I shouldn't have made that choice," but the truth is, God uses all things for our good (Romans 8:28), even what look like mistakes.

Some of the most regrettable times in my life were brought about while making choices that were simply judgment calls; not sin issues. I truly sought to do what I believed God wanted me to do. Looking back, they appear to be mistakes. And the fallout was difficult. I had to apologize; I had to make things right. Some relationships and situations never returned to their original shapes.

But you know what? Having the hard conversations and working through the fallout helped develop me into the (somewhat more) mature person I am today. Without those experiences, I would lack the depth of empathy, understanding, and wisdom I now have when parenting, being a good wife, and leading people. He worked things for good. I wouldn't go back and change those times of character development.

God says, "I have been to your future. It is good. I've come back to take you there."

He knows where He's going. He knows where He wants you to go. Will you trust Him each day to keep you in His good plan? When you get on the People Mover, finding His will isn't all that hard. You just keep your feet planted in Him, and let him take you along good paths.

Prayer

God, I trust that You know the best choice in every decision I must make. I trust that even though I can't see past obstacles, You can. So I stay in faith and remain obedient to Your guidelines in Scripture.

Where there's a judgment call, I submit myself to Your Spirit's leading in me and move forward with confidence in Your ability to take me someplace good.

In Jesus' name, amen.

KELLY DYKSTRA

5

BENEFIT 2:
YOU CAN STOP TRYING SO HARD

Oh, to be normal

Hey Jesus-follower, have you ever felt like the Christian life is exhausting? Do you ever want to just quit? Or quit for a while? To just be (imagine me whispering) *normal* for a little bit?

I mean, come on...

Normal people have bonfires and BBQs.

> You have worship practice and Bible study.

Normal people go out to eat.

You're on a 14-day fast and are seriously considering *eating* a normal person.

Normal people go on vacation.

You gave every penny from your savings account to the church's capital campaign.

Normal people read novels and get lost in a good story.

You read an ancient history book and try to find its hidden meanings for your life.

Normal people dream about retirement.

You dream about dying. (And getting a mansion in heaven, but still, there's the part about dying first.)

There's an old hymn that says something like, "Let me burn out for You, dear Lord..."

As if ultimate success in a Christian's life is to deplete oneself of every ounce of vibrancy, energy, and even functionality, until nothing is left but a charred pile of remains where a person Jesus died to grant abundant life to, used to be.

What if that's not what God intended?

What if the idea of draining our life "for the sake of Christ" is a lie the enemy designed to keep our hopes in *our* efforts instead of *Christ's* efforts in/through us? If

Satan and his servants can make us think that the Kingdom of Heaven can not advance on earth without every second of our time, every calorie we have to burn, and every spare penny in our account, Christians will live a stressed-out, frantic, guilt-ridden life that *no one else is interested in living.*

Let's pause for a moment for a note regarding *a life no one else is interested in living*:

Think about this, because it's important. As true Jesus-followers who have experienced the wonderful Christian life, we want others to experience this relationship with God that we have, right? But when unbelievers look from the outside into our lives, is it attractive? Does it look *better* than what they have? Not, are we rich, skinny and awesome or living lives of hedonistic pleasure; but do we have something more appealing than the lives they currently live?

When he looks at you, does an unbeliever see you *not* indulging in a party lifestyle or pursuing wealth above all else, or doing things he finds enjoyable? If so, he might think, "Wow, they must not have a lot of fun."

And then, upon further examination, he sees that you have replaced selfish pleasures and destructive living with a schedule full of church activities that conflict with every fun thing everyone else is doing, topped with a poverty mentality and martyr syndrome because you're *burning out for Jesus.*

Um, no, thank you.

He might be willing to consider the Christian life if his version of a good life (that maybe deep down he finds meaningless) can be replaced with something he would find valuable (like peace, joy, meaning and purpose in life; healthy relationships, community).

But if, from all external vantage points, your "better" life looks not only *not fun* but also bogged down with obligations and stress and sacrifices, *why would he want to follow your Jesus?!*

Talk about destructive living.

Talk abut a major misrepresentation of the life Jesus died for us to live.

Oh, the insanity

When I look back at my growing up years in a hyper-conservative church in the Deep South, it blows my mind that people would choose to become Christians at our church. The message we sent was, "Come follow Jesus with us. When you do, you'll look like us! We don't drink, smoke, go to movies, swim with the opposite sex, dance, play with playing cards, listen to rock music (or country), or even go to restaurants that play *that music* while we eat."

Follow God, and you get to fill your schedule up with church things. Sunday morning Sunday school hour followed by the worship service. Bible study Sunday evening, followed by a second worship service. Wednesday night church. Thursday night "visitation", where you go (uninvited) to visit people at their homes and talk about faith, and Saturday morning "bus visitation", where you check in on the families of the kiddos the church bus will be picking up on Sunday. (Note: these ministries are valuable. I'm just pointing out the craziness of a person doing ALL of them.)

Congratulations, ladies! If you follow Jesus, you get to throw away all your shorts, jeans and pants, and instead you'll wear below-the-knee skirts or really ugly long split-skirts called culottes that hide all hints of femininity. The neckline of your shirt can't dip below two fingers from your collarbone. (Yes, that was a guide we had.)

Men, you'll need to cut your hair really short and gouge your eye out if you look twice at a woman, because sexual sins are the worst. Well, besides dancing. And I'm pretty sure married people scheduled sex just for procreation. And it was probably done with the lights off.

OK, that last bit was just me being snarky, but you get the point, and even as I type this I am overwhelmed with this thought:

How powerful is God's love for lost people that He even works through our complete and utter mangling of His message of grace! He manages to bring people to Himself despite the way His people misrepresent Him.

None of the above list of rules and church activities is inherently bad. The rules were designed by well-meaning Christians to help themselves stay as far from sin as possible. The church activities were designed to help the people in the church thrive in a community of faith. I get that. I've been known to develop my own list of things I should do—or I think others should do—to thrive spiritually.

I should also mention that as a pastor in a church, I know that the church is a volunteer organization, and we *need* people to serve. And people *need* to serve, because that's why God gave us gifts.

God has given each of you a gift from His great variety of spiritual gifts. Use them well to serve one another. (1 Peter 4:10-11)

Having said that, I wish to return to the point I was making before my rant. If our enemy can make us think that *people will go to hell* and *we aren't good enough Christians* if we aren't checking off every item on the church's list, we will spend our lives committing the original sin (as discussed in Chapter 4): depending upon human effort to achieve godly life.

That's not what Jesus died for.

Breathe

Jesus did not say, "Come to me, and I will take your already overworked, stressed-out life and add a list of approved activities that will make God proud of you."

No. Check out Matthew 11:28-30. *Then Jesus said, "Come to me, all of you who are weary and carry heavy burdens, and I will give you rest. Take my yoke upon you. Let me teach you, because I am humble and gentle at heart, and you will find rest for your souls."*

Stop for a second. Take a deep breath and blow it out. Relax your shoulders. Say aloud, "I don't have to burn out for Jesus." I'm serious. Say it. "I don't have to burn out for Jesus." Break the agreements you've made with the enemy about a need to perform, atone for your guilt, or achieve your own holiness, and agree with the truth Jesus speaks over your life.

Come, step into life with Me, the People Mover. Bring your fatigue and weariness and baggage and the load you carry. Link up with me, like two animals share a yoke and pull together. I'm much stronger, so I can pull even if you need to rest.

But what about backsliding?

Have you heard of backsliding? I remember hearing the term "backslider" and associating it with "leper".

Where's Frank? He hasn't been to church in a few weeks.

He's backslidden.

Pause. Eyes widen, tongue makes that *tsk tsk* noise.

Oh, no. He's a backslider.

He...slid...back.

To where?

I dunno. But he hasn't been coming to church, so he's probably eating at the Pizza Hut, where they serve beer and play rock music on the jukebox.

We don't use the term *backsliding* much anymore, but the underlying thought process remains. If I am not moving forward in my faith, in terms of expectations that the church/other Christians/I have on my life, I'm sliding backward.

We've even preached this in the past. I remember Eric talking about getting his old rusty 1980-something F-150 stuck in the mud because instead of keeping those wheels moving, he let off the gas, slid back, and got stuck.

If you're not moving forward, you're sliding back.

If there's no progress, you'll regress.

Keep. Moving. Keep. Moving. For God's sake, keep moving forward or you'll slide back and have to start over.

But Jesus said, *I offer you rest.*

Well, WHICH IS IT?!!!

If you must keep your foot on the gas, always working for a deeper faith, a more productive Christian walk, the next activity, the bigger sacrifice, you are not on a People Mover.

YOU ARE ON A TREADMILL.

Those are two VERY DIFFERENT pieces of machinery. Conceptually similar, but very different. On a treadmill, you can definitely backslide. It's simple. Just stop trying. You will slide back and land right on your backside.

On a People Mover, the moment you stop trying to move forward in your power is the very moment you demonstrate a complete and total faith in the Mover to take you where you need to go.

Sometimes, your greatest act of faith is to stop trying.

Hurry up and rest

It takes more faith to trust that the work Jesus did was enough to get God's pleasure on your life, than to try to work for it yourself. At least you can *see* the work you're doing. It's pretty tough to always see what Jesus is doing. Dang it, sometimes it's hard to rest! Even the Bible says it's hard.

Hebrews 4:9-11 says, *So there is a special rest still waiting for the people of God. For all who have entered into God's rest have rested from their labors, just as God did after creating the world. So let us do our best to enter that rest...*

Do our best to rest.

I don't know about you, but I find it hard to rest when I know there's work to be done. Going to sleep knowing there are dirty dishes in my kitchen is so difficult for me! I like to lay my head on my pillow feeling like all is right in my home. Sometimes Eric says, "Kelly, you're tired. Just go to bed. The dishes will get done."

I think, "No, they won't. I'm the only one who will do those stupid dishes. Clearly I'm a bad housekeeper and mother because we live in such a pit." And if I insist on rolling my sleeves up and getting to work when I'm already tired and teetering on the edge of martyrdom, doing the work is only going to make it worse. In fact, it will reinforce the idea that *I'm the only one doing any work. I am the answer to everyone's mess in this house.*

The best option is to shove away the lies and force myself to rest. The outcome? Either, a) someone else will do them while I rest, or b) I'll wake up refreshed, realign my heart with God's grace, and get the work done with a better spirit.

Do you find it hard to rest spiritually when you feel like there's so much dirt/mess in your life?

I'm so jacked up, I don't know how I can thank Jesus for forgiving me. I owe Him so much. I should work for Him constantly. I should keep trying to be a better person.

Or worse yet, there's so much dirt/mess in other people's lives, and you know you can help. You have the answer! It's Jesus! But you're so tired.

If I spend another two hours listening to my buddy's dysfunction, trying to give good counsel, trying to keep him sober, I'll be so exhausted I won't have anything left for my wife and kids.

Jesus says, "I offer you rest."

What do you need to *stop* doing for a while, so you can actually enjoy your life? I'm not saying swear off the church or helping people. I'm not saying quit reading your Bible or praying or fasting when you believe God is telling you to.

I'm just asking, what are you doing that you *think* is propelling you forward spiritually, and you're afraid that if you stop, you'll lose your momentum? If you stop, you'll go to hell?

Worse yet, if you stop, someone else will go to hell?

I wish to remind you that Jesus is the Savior, not you.

Do you hear that?

Jesus loves lost people way more than you ever could, so trust Him to care for them when you need to refocus for a bit and care for yourself and your family.

Is your faith misplaced?

Is it in human effort or His effort? You can *say* it's in Jesus, but your actions speak louder than...well, you know the saying.

Are you trusting the People Mover enough that when He says, *rest*, you do it? Shout down the lies that say you'll slide backwards and trust Him to carry your weight and keep moving you forward.

Prayer

Dear Father, Sometimes the compulsive achiever, I find it easier to trust my own efforts than Yours to get stuff done, grow in faith, and help people. Other times, the guilty sinner in me causes me to battle the lies of condemnation by trying to outweigh my guilt with good deeds. Either way, it's a lack of trust in You, pure and simple.

Help me relax in Your care, and live no more in fear of what will happen. I step off the treadmill I've created for myself and onto You, the One who will move me forward even when I rest.

Amen.

6

BENEFIT 3:
YOU CAN TAKE A DAY OFF

A revolutionary concept

After several years of ministry life on the self-effort treadmill, Eric and I found ourselves worn out, unhealthy, struggling in our marriage, and thinking, *there is no way we can do this life long-term.* We knew it wasn't good, but we didn't know the answer. You and I both know the answer now, which is a change of thinking—but in our effort to get healthy, we stumbled across a concept that actually helped us move away from the idolatry of work/progress/success and began to turn our hearts toward dependence on God's ability to get stuff done in, through, and for us.

It's called Sabbath rest.

Entire books have been written on this concept, and I'll not go into loads of theological discussion here. I would like to simply present to you the concept, what it does for our family, and allow you to make a choice for yourself.

Remember to observe the Sabbath day by keeping it holy, is the directive in Exodus 20:8. It's one of the 10 Commandments, but it's not mentioned much, since the results of breaking it aren't immediately obvious.

Thou shalt not kill? Yeah, you break that one—you've ended a life. Bam. Done. It's a death of a person and an immediate stamp on you. *Killer.*

Thou shalt not commit adultery? It affects people. You, the person you're messing with; the one(s) you're betraying; and the others in your life who will be affected by your choices. *Home-wrecker.*

Fail to keep the Sabbath holy? Meh. It's like a little white lie. Wrong, we suppose, because there's a [hypothetical] rule about it, but there is no immediate consequence of breaking the Sabbath. Nobody ever went to jail for Sabbath-breaking and entering. But there must be a reason why God included this directive in His list of laws.

Now, let's pause and clarify that in the New Testament, we learn that Jesus met the demands of the law on our behalf, and His blood paid for our sins.

Galatians 3:23-25 says this.

> *Before the way of faith in Christ was available to us, we were placed under guard by the law. We were kept in protective custody, so to speak, until the way of faith was revealed. Let me put it another way. The law was our guardian until Christ came; it protected us until we could be made right with God through faith. And now that the way of faith has come, we no longer need the law as our guardian.*

I need to be clear that under grace, we are not commanded to keep the law in order to please God. We've been through this already. Jesus pleased God, and God is pleased with us when we put our faith in Jesus.

BUT we can see helpful hints for life (to put it lightly) when we look at the 10 Commandments. The law was a revelation of God's heart to keep His people safe and to keep society from denigration.

So. The Sabbath. One day each week that carries a command. One day that is holy.

Holy. Set apart. One of these days is not like the others. (Thanks, Sesame Street! That song will be stuck in my head for the next few hours.)

The rhythm of rest

Here's the command in context in Exodus 20:8-11.

> *Remember to observe the Sabbath day by keeping it holy. You have six days each week for your ordinary work, but the seventh day is a Sabbath day of rest dedicated to the Lord your God. On that day no one in your household may do any work. This includes you, your sons and daughters, your male and female servants, your livestock, and any foreigners living among you. For in six days the Lord made the heavens, the earth, the sea, and everything in them; but on the seventh day he rested. That is why the Lord blessed the Sabbath day and set it apart as holy.*

God Himself modeled a Sabbath in Creation Week. He was productive for six days, and on the seventh day, He took a break. According to Genesis 2:2-3, He blessed the day. He must have REALLY liked it, for some reason!

So the creation of the heavens and the earth and everything in them was completed. On the seventh day God had finished his work of creation, so he rested from all his work. And God blessed the seventh day and declared it holy, because it was the day when he rested from all his work of creation.

Why did God rest?

It's just silly to think He went to bed the night of Day 6 and thought, "It's been a long, tough week. I'm not going to set my alarm for tomorrow. I could really use a mental health day. A ME-day."

Really? GOD needs a break? A rest? Ridiculous. God did this (and made sure it was documented) to establish a rhythm by which humankind could live.

Day 1 – work

Day 2 – work

Day 3 – work

Day 4 – work

Day 5 – work

Day 6 – work

Day 7 – rest

And then it starts over. Work, work, work, work, work, work, rest.

As God designed the wake/sleep cycle for us to recharge daily, He designed the work/rest cycle for us to recharge weekly. A day that is holy—set apart—for rest. Why is this such a big deal? Besides the obvious benefit of having a day to chill out, the Sabbath has spiritual meaning.

It's an act of faith.

Setting aside a day to relax, enjoy my family, and remember God, is an act of faith that says, "God, even though I have work to do, money to earn, and goals to accomplish, I will rest today. In doing so, I acknowledge that I trust You to get done what needs to get done in my life. I refuse to be fully responsible for my productivity. I believe that as I honor Your plan for my well-being, You will supernaturally advance my work in the other six days."

Tithing time

The Sabbath is like a time-tithe. The tithe as modeled in Scripture is returning to God the first tenth of what He gives us, and choosing to live off the other 90%. It is an act of faith that says, "God, I acknowledge that all I have comes from You. I believe that if I honor You by bringing You the tithe, You will cause the other 90% to be enough to meet my needs."

So the basic tithing equation goes like this:

100% given to me

- 10% back to God, the Giver

100% of what I need.

More than that, He promises that when we tithe, He gives us additional blessings too!

Check out Malachi 3:10-12.

> *"Bring all the tithes into the storehouse so there will be enough food in my Temple. If you do," says the Lord of Heaven's Armies, "I will open the windows of heaven for you. I will pour out a blessing so great you won't have enough room to take it in! Try it! Put me to the test! Your crops will be abundant, for I will guard them from insects and disease. Your grapes will not fall from the vine before they are ripe," says the Lord of Heaven's Armies. "Then all*

> *nations will call you blessed, for your land will be such a delight," says the Lord of Heaven's Armies.*

After reading this, I believe that the tithing equation looks even better than we originally thought:

100% given to me

- 10% back to God, the Giver

>100% [more than] what I need.

In the same vein, when we choose to "tithe" some time to rest in God's rhythm for us, we can anticipate supernatural abundance in our productivity. Because we don't live in just the natural. On the People Mover, we live in the supernatural grace/faith life with Jesus.

So. Choosing to honor a weekly Sabbath day is an act of mercy on our worn-out bodies, minds and emotions after a week of work.

And it's an act of faith that responds to God's love and grace—and His desire to accomplish more through us than we could on our own.

He says, *Cease striving and know that I am God.* (Psalm 46:10, NASB)

It is only in stopping striving that we demonstrate outwardly our internal belief that He is God, and we are not. I'll say it again. By obediently resting, we sit down and allow God to work. We acknowledge that we are not fully responsible for our productivity.

Here's how our life used to work:

168 hours per week

- _0_ hours set aside to honor God in rest

168 hours of us being fully responsible for our own productivity.

And here's how it works now:

168 hours per week

- 24 hours set aside to honor God in rest

168 hours of us trusting God to get everything done.

So what do we get? A break *and* the promise of full productivity!

Funny story? Stuff always gets done.

How freeing!

Practical tips for Sabbath

Eric and I were at a week-long pastors' retreat when we ran across the concept of modern-day Sabbath rest. Not legalistic, Orthodox Jewish Sabbath--like if your donkey falls in a well after sundown the night the Sabbath begins, you have to leave it there--but a grace-filled, here's-what-a-loving-God-offers-us weekly day of rest. We decided to make this a part of our lives, which was a bit challenging at first, because we work weekends. Initially we chose Mondays, as that's when we're most exhausted from the weekend of church. Eventually we switched to Fridays so that we enter into the most important ministry days of our week well-rested.

When you choose a Sabbath, it needs to be intentional, and you will want to communicate about it with people it might affect. You don't want your personal spiritual decision to be a rude jolt to someone who is accustomed to your attention any time they think they need it.

Eventually, we required all of The Crossing Church staff to share the same Sabbath (day off), so no one needs anyone else for work, and we didn't have to keep track of who we shouldn't bother on which days. That's why our offices are entirely closed on Fridays, and if a staff member is caught working, we graciously guide him/her back to a place of faith that God will help them accomplish their work on work days. Almost every time we deal with burnout with a staff member, we find that they have been working on Fridays.

For us, we choose not to answer our phones, check email, or have any sort of work-related conversations. When we first implemented our Sabbath, it required actually turning our phones off. Over time, people stopped calling or texting out of respect for our Sabbath. Now we know that if they *do*, it's likely an emergency. Which is good, because I now leave my phone on due to Sabbath Candy Crush binges. (Don't judge me.)

On our Sabbath, we don't do housework or yard work or discuss our budget or do things that will tire or stress us. We enjoy good food and drink. In years past, I would prepare food ahead of time so that I didn't need to cook. For awhile, we would go out to eat. But most recently, since we go out to eat so much for convenience sake during the work week, I enjoy staying home and cooking on Fridays. We also chose to make our Sabbath a family day in which we do not spend time with other people, for the most part.

We do what makes us happy.

I encourage you to do what makes you happy. If you're

a people-person, maybe you should have a party every Friday. Maybe yard work is relaxing for you. Or de-knotting your necklaces or changing your oil. Only you know what refreshes you, so do what works for you.

Parents, have you ever thought to yourself, "Boy, my kiddo sure is quiet," and you get a little nervous? Then you peek around the doorframe of his room to find that he's playing contentedly with the toys you've given him? Isn't that a good feeling?

I imagine that God sometimes does that. He takes a peek at us and smiles when He finds that we're quietly enjoying ourselves in the environment He's given us.

Sabbath push-back

I'm well aware that a Sabbath almost sounds indulgent. Like taking a spa day when everyone else is at work. It might sound selfish to shut the world out one day each week. Some people might not understand why you say "no" to perfectly good, fun things. They may perceive it as rejection.

"Oh, it's your ME-day," they may say sarcastically. They may be offended that you're not available to them or that you didn't answer their Facebook post or text right away. Sometimes this great act of faith on your part might look like laziness to someone who doesn't understand. They may compare your workload or schedule with theirs and be critical, jealous, or even superior.

But in our experience, God made our workdays more productive, and eventually our happier, healthier selves were the fruit we had to show for our surprisingly difficult choice to honor God by resting one day of our week.

We started observing a Sabbath and NEVER LOOKED BACK. It continues to be one of the greatest decisions we have made in our entire lives.

What if your work schedule doesn't allow a full day "off" each week? Well. Don't you think God knows about your work schedule? How about you begin with a conversation with Him about this? Don't forget that God is totally rooting for you behind the scenes of your life, as you seek to walk in relationship with Him.

Explain to Him what you'd like to do. Remember, He wants you to take a Sabbath even more than you do! Ask Him to help make it happen. See what happens.

Even making a major life change like implementing a Sabbath can be fairly effortless...when you remember that you have supernatural power on your side. Ask for help and do what He tells you to do, step by step. Watch what He does to help You honor Him.

A Sabbath means you can sit down on the People Mover.

Just have a seat!

You might look funny to others, but you and God will have the last laugh.

Prayer

God, I like the idea that I'm free to take a day off.

I commit to taking steps toward clearing a day to be my Sabbath each week.

Please remove the obstacles that I can't, and give me the courage to remove the obstacles I can. I believe that when I honor You by resting on the one day, You'll make the other six more productive. I refuse to be solely responsible for my productivity.

Please show me Your hand at work as I choose to rest.

Amen.

7

BENEFIT 4:
YOU GET SUPERNATURAL
PROPULSION

More bang for your buck

Here's how this (literal) People Mover thing looks for Eric and I, when we go through an airport concourse on a normal day. Anytime (and I do mean every time) I see a People Mover, I get super excited and jump on for the ride. Eric does not.

He says, "I need the exercise."

I say, "I need the exercise too, but I want my exercise

to count for more."

See, if I stand for a ride on the People Mover, I'll move along nicely. But If I decide I'd like some exercise and start walking, every step I take is multiplied, because I'm combining my energy with the People Mover's energy. Together we can really make progress!

I'm not saying I'm smarter than Eric, but I do think my way makes more sense (or at least feels more fun). I like the idea that while I'm taking my steps, the Mover is causing me to zoom toward my destination! An unseen Force advances me faster than I can go on my own. Sometimes my kids and I run on the Mover. That's super fun, because it kind of feels like flying! We run and laugh and shoot out the other end, breathless (and way ahead of Eric).

One of my favorite stories in scripture is in John 6. Here's how the story goes.

> *That evening Jesus' disciples went down to the shore to wait for Him. But as darkness fell and Jesus still hadn't come back, they got into the boat and headed across the lake toward Capernaum. Soon a gale swept down upon them, and the sea grew very rough. They had rowed three or four miles when suddenly they saw Jesus walking on the water toward the boat. They were*

> *terrified, but He called out to them,*
> *"Don't be afraid. I am here!" Then they*
> *were eager to let Him in the boat, and*
> *immediately they arrived at their*
> *destination. (John 6:16-21)*

Did you catch my favorite part? It says *immediately* they arrived at their destination.

Immediately. As in, it took no time at all. Almost as if they had rowed all they way to shore, and Jesus just jumped in at the last second.

But they weren't even close.

If they had been close to shore, they wouldn't have been freaking out. They wouldn't have been afraid they were going to die. And it's likely they wouldn't have even seen Jesus, because their eyes would've been on their destination, pleased with their own personal progress, preparing to head off the water and get out of the storm. They could've even been contemplating jumping out and wading the last few yards.

No, they were out on open water, fearing for their lives. And when they joined forces with the People Mover, He supernaturally propelled them to their destination in the blink of an eye.

Because that's what Jesus does. He's the Miracle Worker. He is supernatural. He is holy. Set apart. Not like us. His ways are higher than our ways. His thoughts are higher than our thoughts. He is able to accomplish way more than we can ask or even imagine! (Ephesians 3:20)

What must have entered the disciples' minds when they realized Jesus was joining them?

Oh, good. It's Jesus.

Maybe He'll multiply the oars and help us row. I saw Him do that with food.

Whew! We'll ask Him to calm the waves.

Maybe He has some leftover bread and fish in His pocket. I forgot to pack a snack, and this trip is taking way longer than I thought it would.

I'm pretty sure not one of them thought something crazy like this:

Oh, good. Jesus is with us. I bet we'll get to shore in—wait for it—three, two...

I'm thinking the disciples didn't even consider asking Jesus to make them *immediately arrive* where they needed to go. I suppose they only expected Him to calm the waves or keep them safe on their journey. Or maybe help them row. They knew Jesus could control the wind and waves, since He'd done it before. They were probably relieved when He got in the boat because they figured He'd settle the sea or at least make them feel better about their circumstances.

Surely they didn't imagine that between one blink of their eyes and the next, they'd be *there*.

Mind-blowing possibilities

How many times have you not even considered asking God to do a legitimate miracle in your situation? Rather, your imagination is limited to asking for peace in the storm. Shoot, anyone skilled in meditation or stress management can conjure up some inner peace in a hard time. But to radically reverse a desperate situation? To overwhelm the circumstances with miraculous change, resolution, transformation?

It doesn't even occur to us to ask.

Help me cope

is your prayer, instead of

Heal my body.

Give me peace

is the cry of your heart, instead of

Change my circumstances.

Let the proceedings go smoothly

rather than

Jesus, stop this divorce.

Give me wisdom to manage my financial crisis

is your prayer, instead of

Free me from debt.

Do you only allow room in your mind and faith for Jesus to do what He's done before in your life, or do you allow for mighty, miraculous, supernatural acts that you haven't even had the nerve to imagine? I'm not discrediting the things He's done in the past. His past miracles or workings in our lives serve to build our faith and help us trust Him for the future. But don't get locked into the idea that Jesus will only do what He has always done.

He is consistent, but He is not predictable.

He can supernaturally advance a process that "typically takes three months," and get you what you need in a week.

He can cause you to walk out of the meeting with not only the account you were going for, but three solid leads for more.

He can prepare a heart so that when you have the difficult conversation, forgiveness is already waiting.

For the undertaking you are dreading, He already has a miracle plan in place.

You do *not* want to miss out.

You're not disqualified

Don't miss out on your miracle just because it doesn't occur to you to ask.

Don't miss out because it *does* occur to you to ask—but you think you don't deserve help.

Don't miss out just because you are where you are because of the choices you've made.

In the past, I've had "oh crap" moments because of my own stupid choices or failures to get it right. And I felt dumb asking God to come and do a miracle for me— because my situation was *my own &*%$ fault.* So why should He rescue me?

I thought, *I was dumb enough to get myself in this spot. I need to do penance for it by figuring out how to get out.*

And then I realized that there is no crisis that hasn't been brought about by somebody's sin, poor decision, or lack of intelligence. Their humanity.

Regardless of why you are where you are, the nature of your good Father God is to meet you there and do something for you that you cannot do for yourself.

For your own sake *and* the sake of His glory, let Him do something AWESOME for you. Don't start by trying to dig yourself out. Start by asking Him to move.

> *I waited patiently for the Lord to help me, and he turned to me and heard my cry. He lifted me out of the pit of despair, out of the mud and the mire. He set my feet on solid ground and steadied me as I walked along...Many will see what he has done and be amazed. They will put their trust in the Lord. (Psalm 40:1-3)*

Notice this doesn't say, "I waited patiently for the Lord to help me, and He started by looking over the edge of my pit and asking, 'Well, how'd you get into *that* mess?'"

Jesus' redemptive work on the cross qualifies us for

God's miraculous work in our lives. And He enjoys doing this because a) He likes seeing His kids succeed, and b) Other people will see miracles and choose to turn to Him as well.

***

Here's a legitimate question for you to consider:

If you can always anticipate, identify, presuppose what God will do--*is He really God?* I'm pretty sure one of the key requirements for being God is *supernatural power.* The ability to come up with and execute plans that are impossible for the rest of us to conceive or birth.

So. If He is actually God—and He's actually *your* God—then here's what you can know. The mysterious, supernatural, over-and-beyond-imaginative, incredibly powerful God is with you, guiding you through life. And you can EXPECT to be abundantly blessed, overwhelmed, awed, and propelled faster, farther than you could ask or imagine.

Sure, maybe you need the exercise. Maybe you have to go through the motions of doing what you have to do, rowing where you have to go, enduring in a storm. But why not join forces with the People Mover *in every circumstance*?

I think you'll find that with each step you take down the path to your destiny, He will advance you with His supernatural propulsion.

Prayer

God, in my journey to get from point A to point B, there are steps I know I need to take. There are struggles I know I will face. But I choose to take each step and face each struggle in Your power and not just my own.

I commit to asking—and expecting—You to supernaturally overwhelm each difficult circumstance with Your brilliant, more-than-I-could-imagine power. I'm excited to see what You do.

In Jesus' name, amen.

8

WHEN THE PEOPLE MOVER STOPS

You thought things were rolling along smoothly, and you had a great ETA on your next goal or dream, and then you heard and felt this nasty grinding sound, and all of a sudden the Mover stopped so fast you fell on your face.

Ever happened to you?

I thought we were finally making progress.

I thought things were looking up!

What on earth happened?

If the stop happened intensely enough, the thoughts might have progressed even more darkly:

I trusted You.

I denied my human effort and chose Your way, and now I'm less successful. In fact, at the moment, I feel worse off than I was before.

What's up with that?

I can't presume to know why the Mover may stop for you at any point, but in my experience, there are a few possible reasons. Maybe one of them is yours.

1) God will sometimes push pause to let us catch up.

Meaning this: If you haven't yet obeyed what He last told you to do, He might pause and give you a chance to obey before He continues moving you forward.

When you feel stuck, stop and think: "What's the last thing I KNOW God told me to do?" Have you obeyed? If He immediately brings something to mind, consider obeying and seeing what happens.

2) Maybe it's a training exercise.

In the military, before one can move on to the next rank, certain training exercises need to be passed. It is assumed that without this training, a soldier won't be qualified to hold the next title. To be responsible for increased influence. In fact, a series of training exercises need to be completed in order. It wouldn't be fair to throw a recruit out of boot camp straight into leadership without granting him the opportunity to learn how to function in that advanced role.

God has a plan of advancement for you. It looks different for every person, of course, but if you are walking in faith and honoring Him, this plan likely includes the following:

☐ more responsibility (I'm assuming this because pretty much all forms of advancement require a larger scope of *life* to manage),

☐ more influence (I'm assuming this because He wants us to influence the world with His love and truth), and

☐ more resources (I'm assuming this because He promises that when we honor Him with our money, He will bless us).

What if He threw you right into this position of increased responsibility without proper training?

The thing about training is that sometimes it's uncomfortable. I mean, ask anyone who's been through Basic Training if it was comfy. They'll laugh in your face.

But ask if they're better off having been through it. Are they tougher? Wiser? More confident? Ready to kick butt and take names? HOOAH! (Yes, I looked up the spelling of the military shout. Yes, I feel like a dork for using it.)

What doesn't kill you makes you stronger.

I know that's trite, but in God's capable hands, every intentional training exercise we survive makes us stronger and more fit for the opportunities to come.

We become stronger in body or stronger in mind.

Stronger in patience or stronger in faith.

If you can make it through a hard situation without giving up hope, without quitting, you can look back and say, "I did that." The next difficult situation won't be so hard because you made it through this one.

Been there, done that.

It is possible that the halt in your progress or the difficult time you're facing is a strengthening experience to prepare you for the *more* that is just ahead.

3) God might be bored.

Maybe your current situation isn't painful; it just seems like you're not getting anywhere. Your job looks like a dead end, but you can't see another option. You're doing the right things but taking no risks in life or faith.

Maybe God's like, "Look, I'm happy to carry you to a good future, but let's have some fun with it." I'm not sure there are major biblical grounds for this one, but let's roll with it for just a minute. What if you're not supposed to live a vanilla life? It's average, it's safe, it's obedient, but there's no real excitement because there's no real risk.

Consider the first disciples of Jesus. These were just normal dudes, cruising along in their normal life, living their normal understanding of faith, keeping the Sabbath, doing the traditional religious sacrifice thing, and pleasing God to the best of their ability. They were engaged in the family business (fishing) with their dad, and along came Jesus (Matthew 4).

He was like, "Hey, come follow me, and I'll show you something cool."

And they were like, "Seeya, Pops!" And they took off with the weird dude. As a result, they got to be a part of the greatest story in human history. They got front row seats to the redemption of humankind.

Maybe you're just a normal Christian, cruising along in your normal life, living your normal understanding of faith, hitting church most weekends, praying, reading your Bible, and sharing your faith when it's convenient. Maybe you're just minding your business riding along on the People Mover, and Jesus is like, "I'm not going to let the gentle forward motion of the Mover rock you to sleep anymore. Wake up!"

What if you looked around to see if Jesus might be standing there with His hand out, saying, "Come follow me, and I'll show you something cool!"?

Will you say yes? I don't know what that might be for you.

Maybe it's a mission trip.

An opportunity to teach a class at church.

An audition for the band.

Volunteering.

Scheduling a coffee date with someone you've been wanting to encourage in faith.

Updating your resume and going after that dream job.

Speaking up about an injustice that burns a hole in your heart.

Bringing the first 10% of your income to the church (tithing).

Going to counseling.

Seeking forgiveness where you've done wrong.

Granting forgiveness for when you've been wronged.

Going to school.

Walking into a recovery meeting.

Inviting someone to church.

Moving across the world.

Your crazy risk might just position you to take your place in the greatest story in human history. You might get front row seats to the redemption of lives around you. You might put into motion a small thing that God propels into something great.

Maybe the Mover stopped to shake up your status quo and show you something that will rock your world in the best way possible.

Don't walk away

Regardless of the reason it seems God brought your forward progress to a screeching halt, the crux of this thing is that you've got to choose to stay on the People Mover anyway. One of the craziest things people do is quit on faith when life gets tough.

As if walking AWAY from the grace and hope and wisdom of Jesus is going to help you get back to a better place in life. [Insert face-palm here.]

When our kiddos were little, we used to occasionally

fight the hold-my-hand battle as we walked through a parking lot. They always wanted to pull away from us and run ahead or away, and, being good parents, we wanted to keep them close to us so we could protect them from harm. We eventually came upon (what we think is) a brilliant strategy. We'd look at the kiddo and say, "Either you can hold my hand, or I can hold your hair. You choose."

Invariably, they'd choose the hand, because who likes being held by the hair? Of course, on occasion, a particularly ornery child (I won't mention names) would call our bluff and say, "Hold my hair!" So we'd have to do it, or else risk blowing the whole thing.

Here's the point: If my child is holding my hand, he can choose to let go and try to get away. But if I'm holding his hair, if he tries to pull away, he will cause himself some pain. I'm not doing it to him; he's doing it to himself by trying to pull away from the one who loves him and wants to protect him.

In the grace of God, we can choose to walk away, but we only cause ourselves more pain. The smartest route is to stay close and let Him hold us when times are hard.

I'm always baffled when someone I haven't seen in church for awhile says to me, "Yeah, I've been going through some stuff, so I stopped coming to church. I stayed away for awhile…"

What. The. Heck.

Let me get this straight: your life starts getting difficult, and the first thing you do is *walk away from the very thing that will get you through the hard times?*

Make the choice to stay

During a difficult time, Eric and I learned a memorable acrostic for FAITH from one of our pastors. It helped us keep our heads up and eyes on Jesus. It helped us stay in faith. Since I don't want to steal his stuff, I've made my own. Here you go.

It's called STAY. To STAY on the People Mover:

S – STICK close to Jesus.

...let us run with endurance the race God has set before us. We do this by keeping our eyes on Jesus, the champion who initiates and perfects our faith. (Hebrews 12:1-2)

Now all glory to God, who is able to keep you from falling away and will bring you with great joy into His glorious presence without a single fault... (Jude 24)

And I am certain that God, who began the good work within you, will continue his work until it is finally finished... (Philippians 1:6)

You made a decision to hook up with the People Mover. Stick with it. Choose to keep up a conversation with Him as you go through each day. Stay in relationship. Ask Him to show you His presence and hand at work in your life. Ask Him for what I call "God-winks" to show you that He is noticing you and working in your life, even though you can't see it.

I do this frequently. When I'm faced with something big that I need God to work on, I ask Him for a wink. And then I look for it. It might be someone buying me coffee or even my child doing the dishes without being told. These little winks keep me aware of His presence and help me stick close to Him.

Also, it helps to continue to worship.

Years ago, a friend lost his wife. When we asked how he survived the pain, he said, "I go in my room and close the door. I put music on, raise my hands, and I just worship Jesus." When you can't control your situation, your best option is to stick freaking close to the One who can.

T – THINK right thoughts.

And now, dear brothers and sisters, one final thing. Fix your thoughts on what is true, and honorable, and right, and pure, and lovely, and admirable. Think about things that are excellent and worthy of praise. (Philippians 4:8)

Think about what you're thinking about. Where does this train of thought take you? Did you just take a ride without considering where it goes? Look ahead down the track. Look at the signs that accompany that route. Will these thoughts lead to depression, despair, anger and bitterness? Make a choice to only jump on trains that take you GOOD places.

Just today, Eric was telling me about a study in which a psychologist directed depressed people to put little colored dots around their home and work space. Every time they noticed a dot, they were to think of a positive thought, idea or possibility. The study involved a few other strategies, but this simple directive helped people prone to negative thinking redirect their trains of thought toward a positive outcome.

When you're in a really dark place, little tools like that will help re-train your thoughts to take you someplace good.

A – AGREE with Scripture.

In dark times, look in Scripture for the good stuff—and agree with what God says. Find the stuff that talks about promises and hope and God's goodness. Stuff like this:

Yet I am confident I will see the Lord's goodness while I am here in the land of the living. Wait patiently for the Lord. Be brave and courageous. Yes, wait patiently for the Lord. (Psalm 27:13-14)

"For I know the plans I have for you," says the Lord. "They are plans for good and not for disaster, to give you a future and a hope." (Jeremiah 29:11)

And this same God who takes care of me will supply all your needs from His glorious riches, which have been given to us in Christ Jesus. (Philippians 4:19)

For I can do everything through Christ, who gives me strength. (Philippians 4:13)

At our church, we say some biblically-based faith statements that go like this.

"I am:

deeply loved,

highly favored,

greatly blessed,

totally righteous, and

destined to reign,

because of Jesus."

It's incredible how agreeing verbally (out loud!) with

God's promises over your life can help keep your faith strong. Maybe you'd like to write these somewhere you will see them and read them aloud as often as you can, until they become part of who you are.

Faith cometh by hearing, and hearing by the Word of God. (Romans 10:17, KJV)

When you agree with Scripture and speak the words of God out your mouth, those words come back into your ears, embedding in your soul and building up your faith.

Y – YELL for help.

First of all, I don't actually mean *yell.* But next time you're writing a book and looking for a verb that starts with y … you'll see why I ended up with *yell.*

Going through tough times stinks. But it stinks worse when you're alone. So yell for help. Phone a friend. Talk to your neighbor. Whatever. Don't do it alone. Even the Lone Ranger had Tonto. Find someone else who is on the People Mover with you, and ask him/her to pray for you and walk with you (or sit with you) during your hard time. That's part of the beauty of being on the People Mover. You move in the company of others going the same direction (more on that in the next chapter).

I'm not saying to bleed all over everyone you meet. I *am* saying you need to get honest about what you're going through with a trusted (believing) friend or two, and borrow some of their faith when yours is wavering.

In Matthew 18:19-20, Jesus said, *I also tell you this: If two of you agree here on earth concerning anything you ask, my Father in heaven will do it for you. For where two or three gather together as my followers, I am there among them.*

When you feel like the Mover has stopped and Jesus is far, gather with a few of His family members and allow them to be the hands, feet, voice of Jesus to you. There is Holy Spirit power in the gathering of His people.

STAY on the People Mover

Stick close to Jesus.

Think right thoughts.

Agree with Scripture.

Yell for help.

Eventually you will see progress.

At just the right time, you'll move forward again.

Prayer

OK, God, I'm choosing to believe today that even when my life doesn't look like I'm making progress, You are up to something good. You are scheming up something awesome that will make my life better and set me up for a good future.

Even when I can't see it, I choose to believe Your words and stick close to You. Philippians 4:6-7 says You give peace beyond comprehension. I trust You for this. I rest in Your peace in this moment.

In Jesus' name, amen.

KELLY DYKSTRA

9

LOVE THE ONES YOU'RE WITH

No matter how opposing their opinions are on a million different things in life, when two people step onto an actual people mover, they are most certainly agreeing on two things:

1. The direction they're headed, and
2. The power that's getting them there.

Barring crazy behavior like running the wrong direction (sometimes my children do this in airports during boring layovers) or ridiculously denying that there's a motor doing the work, all riders on the mover agree on these fundamental points.

One of the huge benefits of choosing to live life in the

family of God is that you're in good company. You aren't alone. You've got a ready-made family of travelers through life. You claim the power of the same blood. You agree on the fundamentals of faith, made the same choice to follow Jesus, and are moving the same direction in terms of desiring to obey God and go where He leads. You won't have to battle opposing ideas or defend your choices.

Or will you?

Anyone who has been a Christian for a while will tell you that Christians are VERY GOOD at fighting over opposing ideas and judging each other over the choices they make. We've got a tainted reputation to overcome when it comes to getting along as one big happy family of God.

I remember hearing my childhood pastor jokingly say at the end of a church service, "Well, we got done early today! We'll beat the Methodists to the restaurant!"

The funny thing is, the reason I was remembering that this week is because of a conversation with a friend who pastors a small rural church. He was telling us that groups from the different churches in town *actually do* sit at Sunday dinner and criticize the other church groups sitting across the restaurant!

Why can't we all just get along? We have the same *blood.*

I believe it's because we think everyone else should abide by our version and understanding of faith.

This isn't totally crazy. I mean, when you experience something good, you like to share it with others. Last week our small Minnesota town got our first sushi restaurant. Saturday night, Eric and I had dinner there after church and have not shut up about it since. *You have to go there! The Happy Hour specials are amazing! Get the shrimp tempura roll! What? You don't like sushi? Try it anyway. It's life-changing. You. Must. Go. To. This. Restaurant. Heck, we'll take you. We'll even buy…*

That's just sushi.

If you have wrestled through a major faith-altering concept and made a decision about how you believe God wants you to handle it, it stands to reason that you will enthusiastically encourage others to choose the same.

Or disagree with those who do not.

And maybe let them know they're wrong.

Out of love and concern, of course.

Yes, I am being sarcastic.

Huh. Just two days ago I was "coached" that I am too sarcastic on the platform in church. Maybe the guy had a point.

~sigh~

There's a very big difference between concern for someone's soul and concern for their total agreement with you in doctrine, worship, lifestyle, parenting, philosophy of ministry (for those who serve—as all should, really—in the local church), entertainment, brand of coffee, *ad nauseum*.

Common ground

The Gospel message.

The Good News that brings us salvation.

This is the foundation on which we agree to stand.

In I Corinthians 15:1-4, Paul gives us a reminder.

> *"Let me now remind you, dear brothers and sisters, of the Good News I preached to you before. You welcomed it then, and you still stand firm in it.* **It is this Good News that saves you if you continue to believe the message…** *I passed on to you what was most important and what had also been passed on to me.* **Christ died for our sins**, *just as the Scriptures said.* **He was**

buried, and He was raised from the dead on the third day, just as the Scriptures said." (Emphasis mine)

This is what I see:

A. Believe you're a sinner, and that Christ died for your sins.
B. Believe God raised Him from the dead, proving His deity and power.
C. Live like you continue to believe that message.

Then he brought them out and asked, "Sirs, what must I do to be saved?" They replied, "Believe in the Lord Jesus and you will be saved…" (Acts 16:30-31)

Those verses and many others cause me to believe that anyone who believes and lives the Gospel (Good News!) is my family, regardless of their choices beyond that initial commitment to follow Jesus.

Honestly, it's not even my job to evaluate whether someone is actually a Christian. If they claim Jesus, I have no other way or right to determine whether their soul is truly "saved", as the old-schoolers say. The true state of their hearts is known only by God Himself. Jeremiah 17:9 says that no one can really understand someone's heart.

2 Corinthians 13:5 cautions: *Examine yourself and see if your faith is genuine.*

Last time I checked, it didn't say, "Examine your brother

and see whether *he* is who he claims to be." Sounds to me like we're each responsible for the authenticity of our own faith.

Here's a reasonable question, though. Are there Christians who don't ride on the People Mover?

Meaning, are there people *in our family* who do not have a concept of *faith can be virtually effortless*?

Yep. Heck, I was one of them.

As we discussed back in the beginning, each believer has a choice to step on the People Mover or retain the world's way thinking and fight his way along through the crowds; through life.

Many, many (way too many) Christians retain this thinking that a life of faith is hard. That the directive in I Peter 1 to *...be holy in everything you do, just as God who chose you is holy,* is totally up to them! And they live in a cycle of victory and guilt, depending on their performance each day.

They see the instruction but miss the empowerment!

Let's take a look at that verse in context. Here's most of I Peter 1:13-25, and I'll insert my insights as we go along. Here we go.

So think clearly and exercise self-control... (v.13)

Once again, it starts with the MIND.

So you must live as God's obedient children. Don't slip back into your old ways of living to satisfy your own desires. You didn't know any better then. (v. 14)

Before Christ, you thought you had to meet your own needs and find your own fulfillment. You didn't know better then, but now you do: God will do this FOR you!

But now you must be holy in everything you do, just as God who chose you is holy. For the Scriptures say, "You must be holy because I am holy". (v. 15-16)

If a holy God chose to make you holy, then it stands to reason that surely you <u>must</u> be holy! If not, then either He has failed to make you holy, or you have failed to let Him!

For you know that God paid a ransom to save you from the empty life you inherited from your ancestors...it was the precious blood of Christ, the sinless, spotless Lamb of God. (v. 18-19)

He paid the price to rescue you from the world's chaos and place you on the People Mover.

Through Christ you have come to trust in God. And you have placed your faith and hope in God because He raised Christ from the dead... (v. 21)

Trust His resurrection power to let you walk in life!

You were cleansed from your sins when you obeyed the truth, so now you must show sincere love to each other as brothers and sisters. Love each other deeply with all your heart. (v. 22)

The truth is: you put your trust in Jesus for salvation. Because you've been made holy, love each other deeply as family.

It's like Peter knew that we'd be inclined to correct everyone else's way of life, so he reminded us that God makes us holy through Jesus. He wraps this whole section up by saying we need to LAY OFF hating on each other and love like family.

How can we say we are about God's kingdom and then intentionally divide it against itself with our negative words?

Any kingdom divided by civil war is doomed. A town or family splintered by feuding will fall apart. (Matthew 12:25)

Immediately, my knee-jerk reaction is to be SUPER annoyed with judgmental Christians when I read this. How about you?

Don't let 'em harsh your mellow

I'm a little afraid that you might have this scenario in your mind:

Picture you.

Happy in God's grace, riding on the People Mover of Jesus' love and power, embracing all who choose to ride with you and calling out lovingly to those who need what you have. Butterflies flit around your head, and flowers pop up on the People Mover as you float along.

But then.

You look out on the world and see other Christians, stuck in their list of rules and efforts to make themselves holy. You feel their disapproving glares as you thrive in joy and freedom from bondage to self-effort.

You frown.

Aren't we supposed to be about love?

"Your love for one another will prove to the world that you are my disciples." (John 13:35)

You see them whispering about you and pointing.

They tweet jabs about your philosophy of grace.

They might even write blog posts about your church or your pastor.

You feel the heat rise in your spirit.

You start formulating retorts, defenses, lists of scriptures.

Ammunition to fight against their attacks.

Those Christians are making us all look bad.

The poison spreads through the Body of Christ.

And you begin to judge them as much as you think they are judging you.

They're missing the truth, though, you argue, *and they're alienating those who need Jesus most! I have a righteous anger!*

Maybe.

But *they* probably think *you're* missing the truth and misrepresenting Jesus. They think *their* anger is justified.

And the second you judge them, you're placing your own rules and requirements (law) on their faith journey.

Don't be guilty of the same sin.

Relax.

Besides, who are you to tell someone else how to live?

Who am I?

Ultimately, we each stand before God alone, under the blood of Jesus.

Everyone's welcome at the foot of the cross

Regardless of where anyone is with the life of grace and the People Mover, we need to remember that in the family of God, we all find common ground at the foot of the cross.

If by some chance you wholeheartedly disagree with my premise, my use of scripture, my logic, or my heart, please know that I love you anyway. I invite you to kneel with me at the feet of Jesus. Acknowledge with me that He alone is our salvation, and His blood flows over and through us. This makes us siblings in the family of God. Siblings disagree, sometimes strongly;

sometimes to the extent that time together is too uncomfortable to be endured often. But we're still family, with one Father and one Brother who paid the price for our adoption.

For God knew his people in advance, and he chose them to become like his Son, so that his Son would be the firstborn among many brothers and sisters. (Romans 8:29)

God decided in advance to adopt us into his own family by bringing us to himself through Jesus Christ. (Ephesians 1:5)

Fellow People Mover riders, don't let your God-given shift in thinking get twisted and become a tool for the enemy to cause division in the family of God. Rather, choose to relentlessly eradicate animosity on any level, and fiercely hold on to love regardless of how other Christians handle your choices.

You won't let them pull you back into self-effort thought.

Don't force your freedom on them.

Don't become angry when they don't understand.

Love.

At the Last Supper, Jesus said this *to his disciples* about how they should treat *each other*. Not how they should treat unbelievers, but how they should treat *each other*, for the *sake* of unbelievers:

So now I am giving you a new commandment: Love each other. Just as I have loved you, you should love each other. Your love for one another will prove to the world that you are my disciples. (John 13:34-35)

Love the ones you're with.

Prayer

Jesus, let me not get dragged into thoughts and arguments whose fruit is division and a bad reputation for Your people. Let me always bring peace and love even to other believers who do not think the same way.

Above all, let our love for each other (despite our differences) model Your love in our world.

Amen

10

INVOLVE GOD

OK, great, you may be thinking. I get the People Mover concept. I made a choice to do life with Jesus. I trust Him to take me where I need to go, but how do I make this change in thinking permanent? How does it become a part of who I am? It's way too easy to just go about life and forget. To slip into old ways of thinking. To go down old paths of behavior. How do I keep from flopping wildly off-and-back-on the People Mover every few days?

It's easier than you think.

It's summed up in two words.

Involve God.

In any given moment, any situation, or even any train of thought... *involve God.*

In the early light of morning.

Involve God.

In the search for your missing wallet.

Involve God.

As anger flares in an unjust moment.

Involve God.

When the numbers don't add up.

Involve God.

When the numbers do add up.

Involve God.

As you peel an orange.

Involve God.

As you empty the dishwasher.

Pump gas.

Wash your car.

Negotiate a contract.

Greet a loved one.

Grieve a loved one.

Plan your vacation.

Plan for retirement.

Plan your week.

Plan your lunch.

Involve God.

When you're on the last life in your guilty-pleasure video game.

Involve God.

When you're taking your last breath in real life.

Involve God.

He is always with you. He is always rooting for you. He is unceasingly interested in you. He is powerfully fighting for you. He is deeply in love with you.

He smiles when He thinks of you. His goodness and mercy follow you around. His favor rests on you. His righteousness marks you.

Involve God.

Do not forget.

Though the world weighs down your shoulders, though cares crush in, He is the lifter of your head.

Involve God.

Do not wait until you are desperate.

Do not delay until there's a disaster.

Do not save Him for search and rescue.

Engage Him ahead of time for planning and protection.

It's our tendency to forget to involve God until we can't possibly think of anything else humanly possible to do.

There's nothing left to do but pray.

Why do we wait until there's nothing *left* but involving

God?

Why don't we involve Him first before we even bother trying? We could save a lot of time, stress, energy, anxiety, frustration, and the list goes on...if we started moving with the People Mover.

For the rest of this book, I'm going to give you some practical ways to involve God in your day-to-day life, which will help your thinking be (and stay) renewed.

A preemptive strike

Let's start with a daily habit of involving God in your day, right away in the morning.

Do you ever lie in bed in the morning, and before you even open your eyes, you mentally go through the list of all your cares and responsibilities that day—or in life in general? I realized that I do this daily. Almost like I am giving myself a morning briefing of all the things I should be worried about.

Last week I caught myself doing this. I even had this image in my mind. I was standing there with a bunch of small boxes. Each box was an area in my life that I needed to handle. As I went through the list, I picked up the boxes and stacked them on my shoulders.

Last week the list looked like this:

- ☐ Plan the marriage retreat.

- ☐ Plan the kids' meals during our trip to Houston.

- ☐ Work on our new campus lease agreement and advertising.

- ☐ Holland's eye appointment. (She texted me, "MOM. I AM BLIND. I can't see people's faces." Who can handle that kind of pressure?)

- ☐ Aidan's book cover.

- ☐ Braden's college scholarship application.

- ☐ Eric. (In general, he's a lot to handle!)

- ☐ Go to the gym.

- ☐ Finalize the church budget for board review.

- ☐ Write a job offer for a new worship leader.

- ☐ Deal with the pork ribs in the fridge before they rot.

- ☐ Work on this book, or it will never. get. done.

- ☐ Do yoga to de-stress (New Year's resolution).

And it went on…and on…and on…

I had so many boxes! Then I stopped.

Why am I picking these up and putting them on my own shoulders? God can handle every single one for me.

Give all your worries and cares to God, for He cares about you. (I Peter 5:7)

So I changed—renewed—my thinking. And I involved God.

I picked up each box and handed it to Him.

One by one, I asked Him to streamline, give wisdom, provide for, direct, remind me, propel me, and give me joy in the process.

What if you started your day with a preemptive strike against all the cares and concerns, the responsibilities and the challenges?

Imagine how much more productive you could be if you involved God right away, before you waste a bunch of time trying to manipulate or manufacture what He can manage on your behalf.

It's wise to spend a little time in God's Word in the morning.

Why?

Because it's a constant source of truth and hope in a stormy world. I'm not talking about a 45-minute Bible study. I'm talking about taking a few minutes to find a solid piece of truth. That reminder or promise or truth (whatever He shows you) can be something you use later in the day to "encourage yourself in the Lord" as King David did in scripture. It might be something you use in prayer or just something that gives you a fresh perspective on God.

While you dress for the day, you can listen to podcasts or talks from pastors across the country. You can work your way through a book that inspires you spiritually (like this one!). Look up the verses that are mentioned, and explore the surrounding context. Personally, I use a journal. I don't write much. I have a little system that I use. Maybe you could try it.

Pause – Read – Ramble – Pray

Pause: Involve God in your time with Him. Ask Him to show you something that will encourage or inspire you.

Read: Read a section of scripture, and feel free to stop when something pops out at you.

Ramble: Jot down a few notes about what you read, what it made you think, and even what's on your mind for the day.

Pray: Talk to God about what you learned or heard, and ask Him to be involved in your day.

Practical tips for newbies

#1 It's important to ask God to talk to you as you sit down to read your Bible. Often people complain that they don't "get anything" out of the Bible, but it never occurs to them to ask God to show them something! Ask Him to give you a "word for the day," and then dig in with expectation.

#2 Where to read tends to be a biggie for those who are new to scripture. Heck, I'm old to scripture, and sometimes I don't know where I feel like reading. You might consider a Bible reading guide like the one included in the Life Journal or a Bible in a Year reading plan. My only caution about those is that it sometimes feels like an agenda that you need to complete each time you sit down to read the Bible. Then you're back to a checklist for being "spiritual." Consider using reading guides as a starting place but don't try to *accomplish* all the reading. Just stop when God shows you something cool.

#3 Write something down. I like to write in my Bible. I circle and underline words and phrases that stick out to me. Later, when I look for places to read or study, I get to review what I've learned before.

I strongly encourage you to use a journal. I totally get that many people hate journaling. Let me just say that it is pretty cool to look back and see the thoughts I've had over the years as I've read my Bible. It's a good reminder that God has talked to me a lot in the past, and it gives me hope when it feels like He's quiet.

For you overachievers, don't you dare freak out and quit if you miss a day. Relax. You will NEVER journal every single day. Fuhgeddaboutit. I release you. Just do it when you do it, and don't feel guilty or annoyed with yourself when you don't. Some days I write the date, get distracted, and never write anything else. It's OK! God doesn't give out gold stars for great work or F's for incomplete papers. He's just happy with you because of Jesus!

#4 Regarding prayer, it's important to talk to God before you move on with your day. This is a relationship you're working on. It's a two-way conversation. Imagine going on a date and not talking. Or having a lovely date but not saying thank you or goodbye—just wandering apart at the end of the night. How strange would that be?

Make sure to respond to what He said through His Word and through His Spirit in your heart. Don't leave Him hanging!

God wants to be involved in your life, but He won't force His way in. It's your choice. I encourage you to choose to involve God right away each morning. Don't wait until 4 pm and then feel dumb because you forgot to involve Him until everything got crazy.

Connecting with God first thing each morning is the smartest, best, most logical way to keep your mind fixed on Jesus. Starting your day on the People Mover is far easier than waiting until you're frustrated, over-whelmed, confused, or annoyed and then making your way over to collapse on the Mover in defeat.

Renew your mind in the morning; step on the Mover. Involve God. You will set yourself up for success as you proceed throughout your day.

Our friend Branden is an owner and Director of Operations for several restaurants. This past Sunday, he gave us some tickets so Holland and I could take my nieces to Frozen on Ice. I didn't get to see him, because he had to leave for a work emergency. He later sent me a text. I got permission to slip it into the end of this chapter.

Here's Branden's story:

> *This week has been a struggle for me professionally. It ended with today's fiasco of me showing up to go to [church] and my phone blowing up about a power outage at one of our locations and our glycol machine starting on fire.*
>
> *Anyway, back to the beginning.*

On my personal daily leadership focus, I tell myself to be the better part of someone's day. I got to Wednesday and realized I'm not usually viewed as the deliverer of good news—so trying to relate that to "being the better part of someone's day" is a struggle.

Wednesday on my drive to the office, I found myself changing up my daily prayer a bit and asked Jesus for His guidance and help on being the better part of someone's day.

Shazammm! Literally minutes later, things started happening. I was blessed with 16 tickets to a Minnesota Wild game, that I gave away to several of our staff. End of year reconciliations finally got finished, and I was able to distribute $32,000 in bonuses (compared to nothing last year at this time). Your tickets came through, a gift certificate showed up, a support vendor came through for me on a $20,000 donation to a charity fund for one of our staff that just had a stroke.

As I sat driving in my car, frustrated that I had to leave church and not attend service this morning, I rewound my week in my head, and the first thing that came to mind was, being the better part of someone's day is really the best part of my day.

Isn't that a beautiful example of how we can try really hard on our own, but the moment we choose to involve God, we see *incredible* things happen?

Branden had a good habit of positive "self-talk" each day, but the day he decided to involve God in his daily efforts and goals, he saw incredible things happen in such quick succession, that there was no question Who was getting things done for him.

Prayer

God, it is so cool that You WANT to be involved in my day! You say that You even know how many hairs are on my head, so I guess the details of my life don't bore You.

Help me remember to start out with You and not to wait and use You for emergency assistance only. I want to live in relationship with You. I choose to involve You.

Take the load I carry. Open doors, give good ideas, pour out blessings. I'm excited to see what You do as I involve You! In Jesus' name, amen.

11

BEFORE YOU GO

Please do church

Most people imagine their faith journey happening mostly in a church. When you hear words like *Christianity*, *faith, worship, God, Bible,* do you picture a worship service, a pastor, a sermon, a church building? That's normal. It's often a church service where we have pivotal faith moments, epiphanies, where we are called to a choice and make a decision to follow Jesus.

It's an oasis where we find refreshment after a long week of depletion.

It's a family reunion; a social club; a concert; a motivational talk; an injection of inspiration; a breath of fresh air; an hour of free childcare; a volunteer opportunity.

It may provoke change; invoke guilt; introduce knowledge; impart wisdom.

Church is many things to many believers.

But when I ask someone how they're doing with God, they *almost always* tie their answer to whether or not they've been in church.

"Hey, how are you doing in faith?"

"Well, I haven't been in awhile."

"Been where?"

"Y'know. Church. I've been busy..."

"Right. But how are you and God?"

~blank stare~ "Uh..."

A relationship with God does not equal church attendance.

But.

The first thing people tend to do when they fall away from faith is walk away from church.

The first thing people tend to do when they walk away from church is fall away from faith.

I hope you never try to separate your faith from church.

No, church is not the source of faith.

It is not where you have to go to meet with God.

It doesn't make you holier.

But the Church of Jesus Christ is the only institution He established while He was physically present on Earth.

When His time here was done, Jesus left to prepare a place for us to spend eternity with Him (John 14:1-3), but He did not abandon us. He sent His Spirit to live in us, guiding, comforting, convicting and empowering us.

And He left His church.

His church: a place we gather in His name and in His presence. *For where two or three gather in my name, there am I with them.* (Matthew 18:20, NIV)

His church: a place we agree together in prayer and see our prayers answered. *I also tell you this: If two of you agree here on earth concerning anything you ask, my Father in heaven will do it for you.* (Matthew 18:19, NIV)

His church: a place to get honest and experience healing. *Confess your sins to each other and pray for each other so that you may be healed. The earnest prayer of a righteous person has great power and produces wonderful results.* (James 5:16)

The church is a thriving oasis in a dry world. When you choose to put your roots down in a healthy local church, you will grow. You will flourish. Your faith will be challenged and your knowledge and wisdom enriched.

The righteous will flourish like a palm tree, they will grow like a cedar of Lebanon; planted in the house of the Lord, they will flourish in the courts of our God. (Psalm 92:12-13)

To keep it in the perspective of this book: if you want to stay on the People Mover, try sticking around the airport.

Body building

Over the course of my life, I've known a few people who referred to themselves as Christians, who insisted that they didn't need church to nurture their faith. I completely disagree.

The church is the body of Christ. We are His hands and feet doing the work of the Kingdom. Each of us is a part of the body, and body parts aren't meant to flop around alone.

1 Corinthians 12:12-27 describes this awesomely.

> *The human body has many parts, but the many parts make up one whole body. So it is with the body of Christ...Yes, the body has many different parts, not just one part...*

> *...But our bodies have many parts, and God has put each part just where he wants it. How strange a body would be if it had only one part! Yes, there are many parts, but only one body. The eye can never say to the hand, "I don't need you." The head can't say to the feet, "I don't need you."...*

> *All of you together are Christ's body, and each of you is a part of it.*

Isn't that cool? It's basically saying, no matter who you are, if you are in Christ, you are a *valuable* part of the body of Christ. You matter! You're specifically designed to fit into your church and to play your part in helping the body thrive.

Pick and stick

It's important to find a church that fits you. If you're a rock'n'roll kind of person, maybe a high church style won't fit you. If you're a postmodern spiritual kind of person, you might cringe in a loud church. Visit churches. Ask God to guide you to the one that will feel like home to you.

Churches are kind of like cola. There are many flavors: regular, cherry, caffeine free, diet, "zero", lime, diet with lime, vanilla, and on it goes. But underneath it all, the basic concept remains the same: it's carbonated cola.

Try the different flavors of church in your area, but be sure that the basic concept remains the same: the Good News is preached, and Jesus is Lord. Wherever you find a good fit for your family, I challenge you to commit and settle in.

It's kind of like marriage. (Not entirely; but kind of.) The church is called the bride of Christ. Choose to love the bride. It's a commitment. Emotions about the bride will change, but the commitment holds even if the emotions shift.

Here are a few suggestions for receiving the fullest benefits from being part of the church:

1. Make an intentional decision to become an active member of your church family. Don't put yourself in the position of having to decide, week after week, whether or not you want to attend. If you do, you will tend to be ruled by the emotions of the moment. Choose. Commit. Stick.

2. Make a choice to follow the leadership of your pastor, and choose to bring him/her honor. If you don't like the pastor, leave and find one you can agree with. It is natural for a church to reflect its leadership, and it is not going to change to accommodate your preferences.

3. Bring people to church. The biggest boost your faith can get is bringing others to Jesus. As you lead others to Him, your maturity grows. It's like becoming a parent!

4. Give. You know the verse about where your treasure is, your heart is? Well, it's true. You value what you invest in. I'd guess about 90% of the Christians who leave our church were never committed givers. If you have invested significantly in something, you're more likely to have a connection and passion for its success and effectiveness.

You can do whatever you like. But after nearly 20 years in ministry, believe me when I say that as a member of the family of God, the happiest place to be is firmly planted in His house.

Remember the people I mentioned who didn't "need" church? I should also mention that they tended to exhibit these characteristics:

-- They were kind of weird.

-- They always appeared a little bit prideful (Let's face it: an "I don't need you" attitude never comes across as humble and Jesus-like).

-- They had dysfunctional lives and often seemed like they carried a martyr complex.

I wonder: if they had allowed themselves to be embraced by the rest of the body of Christ, would they have found joy and encouragement? Would their lives look different today, with healthier marriages and happier families?

Hebrews 10:25 says, *And let us not neglect our meeting together, as some people do, but encourage one another, especially now that the day of his return is drawing near.*

As the world grows more and more unstable, crazy, and violent, we long for the return of Christ Jesus to set things right. His return draws near. This verse says that in the meantime, in the waiting, we gather as His body to worship, encourage each other, and unite as a force to reach as many as we can before our opportunity is gone.

Do not, for the love of God and His lost children, neglect going to church and investing your time, talents and treasure in His Kingdom. You can't go wrong when you value what Jesus values.

Prayer

As independent as I sometimes am, God, I want to be in the place You value—in Your house.

Please help me find a place where I fit, and empower me to commit to stay so that I may thrive in the part I play.

Give me the grace to choose commitment over emotion. Please develop in me a fierce love for Your church and Your family.

In Jesus' name, amen.

12

OK, THIS IS THE END

The big question

As I finish writing and you finish reading, I wish to pose this question: what will change when you go back to your life?

This is one of my favorite questions to ask Eric when he and I are on our way home from a conference, road trip, or even vacation. I invariably look at him and say, "So! What's going to be different when we go home?" There's just something about getting away or gaining new knowledge or having an experience, that I do not want to waste.

I hate the idea of being exposed to *any* potentially life-changing opportunity and missing the impact it could have on my future.

After every conference we attend, we distill our notes down to a list of action steps. Often, concepts from books we read end up on our bathroom mirror so we can keep them in front of our eyes and let the truth develop our faith.

Many years ago, after a weeklong trip to a pastors' retreat center, we made the choice to implement family dinner and a Sabbath. Another time, after staying in a cabin for a week with a limited amount of clothing, dishes and kitchen utensils, we made the choice to get rid of a bunch of excess household items. I realized life was simpler when I was faced with fewer options and less stuff to manage.

The key is that we *intentionally choose* to make positive changes based on what we learn.

How about you? God takes you through experiences… good and bad…so that you may emerge, changed. If you keep your eyes open for the things He wants to teach you, you can then take what you've learned and translate it into a change in thinking, behavior, or pattern moving forward.

And we know that God causes everything to work together for the good of those who love God and are called according to his purpose for them. (Romans 8:28)

Are you His? Have you made the choice to put your life in God's hands?

Have you responded to His call to live according to His purpose for you?

In that case, you are guaranteed that *everything* God allows you to experience *will* serve to carry out His purpose in your life. It sets you up for your destiny. To accomplish the things He knew way ahead of time that He wanted you to do. To thrive in the unique way you are created and formed, taught and developed. It's all a part of the big, beautiful picture!

Now, I'm not saying that every time you stub your toe or find a good parking place, you should be looking around to figure out God's higher purpose in the moment.

Some Christians see a demon behind every bush, and walk around blaming Satan and his workers for every bad thing that happens. Others get kind of fruity about coincidences (or "God-incidences") and almost idolize providential events over God. Let's not focus on the situation and miss the Situator. (That's not a word, but I like it.) This isn't about trying super hard to find significance that may not be there.

But you have experiences. You go places. You learn things.

You read this book.

It's not that the book was brilliant or life-altering. But you've got a fair amount of biblical truth in your hand, right this minute. Regardless of what you've learned (or not), there's a reason you are here in this moment. And God says that when His truth goes out, it won't be stamped void and returned to the Sender. His Word doesn't bounce like a bad check. He's always good for what He signs His name on.

Isaiah 55:11 says, *So shall my word be that goeth forth out of my mouth: it shall not return unto me void, but it shall accomplish that which I please, and it shall prosper* in the thing *whereto I sent it.* (KJV)

Through this book, God has sent you a word. Will you let it take root and prosper in you? You have a choice about whether you'll receive the message and let Him use this experience as seed that will grow and effect change in your life. Or you can just shrug your shoulders and say, "That was nice," and go back to the same ol' same ol'.

James 1:21b-24 describes this in a practical sense.

> *...humbly accept the word God has planted in your hearts, for it has the power to save your souls. But don't just listen to God's word. You must do what it says. Otherwise, you are only fooling yourselves. For if you listen to the word and don't obey, it is like glancing at your face in a mirror. You see yourself,*

walk away, and forget what you look like.

Do you have a humble heart to receive and lean into what God wants to do in, for, and through you, or will you resist it, say, "Talk to the hand," and walk away?

What do you see?

Return for a moment to my opening story about running through the airport. Remember my anxiety, panic, fear and exhaustion? And then there was the moment when I saw the people mover, chose to jump on, and relief came.

When you honestly examine your life, what do you see?

Are you...

Running frantically or cruising gratefully?

Sweating and swearing or resting and blessing?

Glaring and judging or smiling and loving?

Striving or trusting?

Worrying or believing?

What is in the mirror? Do you like what you see? Would you like it to change?

Change starts in the mind.

Romans 12:2 says, *Do not be conformed to the pattern of this world, but be transformed by the renewing of your mind.*

You can start today with a renewed mind, making an overarching, broad-scale decision to step onto the People Mover…Jesus…and let Him carry you to your destiny under His power and not your own.

But you can also make changes in specific areas of your life. Systematically, you can choose to load each area onto the People Mover and submit them to the wisdom and power of Jesus to handle for you. Today, before you walk away from the mirror, make a list of each area you believe has been "conforming to the [crazy] pattern of the world," and choose to involve God in all those areas.

And finally

May you start each day with a mind like-new.

May you find yourself in the company of a family of faith.

May you fly toward your destiny under supernatural

propulsion.

May you believe in God's goodness even if you don't see progress.

May you rest and trust that you will still move forward.

May you involve God and see Him bless every area of your life.

May you experience a life of effortless faith.

And may you share it with others so they can too.

KELLY DYKSTRA

SHOUT-OUTS

Eric, thank you for puuuuushing me to do hard things and for having the courage and wisdom to lead me. I shudder to think where I'd be without you. You and Jesus are the reasons I walk tall (well, also good high heels). You're my favorite. I REALLY like you.

Braden, thanks for being soawesome@gmail.com. You've turned out quite nicely. You are a wise, calm leader. You're also much taller than me now, which is weird. I'm proud to be your mom.

Holland, thanks for thinking I'm still cool enough to take #selfies together. I admire you. It's rare to find such a young woman with the grace and confidence that you have. With the power of Jesus, you will most certainly twirl your world.

Aidan, my creative genius, thanks for keeping me on my toes for nearly 13 years now. I believe that the dreams God has placed in your heart will come true as you live in faith. Make sure you give me a shout-out when you play the Garden. [Aidan is the author of **World War Cheese**, available on Amazon.]

Tracy, you're brilliant. Thank you for so gracefully navigating our multi-faceted relationship. You know me best and seem to like me anyway. Thank you for sticking with me all these years. Let's become little old ladies together and play Scrabble in our robes and slippers.

Katie & Chrissie, I'm so proud of both of my baby sisters. You're smart and beautiful, hardworking and hilarious. We should hang out more. And get more matching tattoos. But next time we won't tell Mom & Dad.

Mom & Dad, thank you for bringing me up in the ways of Jesus. I believe that the billions of seeds you've planted over a lifetime of self-sacrificial ministry and generosity will generate a harvest that is beyond imagination. I love you.

ABOUT ERIC & KELLY DYKSTRA

Eric and Kelly co-pastor The Crossing Church in Elk River Minnesota, which they founded in 2004. With campuses in several cities, The Crossing is seeking to thrill people with God's grace and move them to life in Christ.

Eric is the author of **Grace on Tap** and **Unhooked & Untangled: Finding freedom from your addictions, vices and bad habits.** Both are available on Amazon. His caffeinated teaching style engages even the most skeptical listeners and inspires people at all stages of faith. You can find his sermons at freegrace.tv or on The Crossing Church smartphone app.

Kelly created **The Simple Journal: A starting place for encountering God**, modeled from her own personal journal, to help people begin a habit of spending a few minutes with God each day. Kelly's down-to earth, straightforward preaching enables her to connect with a wide range of audiences. Find her sermons and her "Twirl" events for women at freegrace.tv. She occasionally blogs at KellyDykstra.com. Find her on Twitter and Instagram @KellyDykstra.

Raised in Alabama, Kelly is a southern girl at heart. She finds great delight in olives, Mexican food, coffee, traveling, great high heels, and eating out with Eric and their three children: Braden, Holland and Aidan.

ABOUT THE CROSSING CHURCH

The Crossing started as a "church for people who don't 'do' church." It presently has campuses in Elk River, Zimmerman, Big Lake, and St. Cloud, Minnesota. Find times and locations or attend the online campus at freegrace.tv.

Guilt Free. Grace Full.

The Crossing offers recovery meetings to walk with you as you find freedom from any addiction or struggle. Find times and locations at freegrace.tv.

The Crossing College offers a Diploma in Biblical Studies and an Associates Degree in Church Leadership and Ministry. The mission of the college is to equip God's people with His wisdom for life, to know how to read, understand and apply the Bible, and to live life to the fullest with Jesus. Find more information at TheCrossingCollege.com.